SUCCEEDING IN SPITE OF EVERYTHING

Presented by Sandra Yancey

D1041744

Presented by: Sandra Yancey

Producer: Ruby Yeh

Editorial Director: AJ Harper

Print Management: Book Lab

Cover Design: eWomenNetwork

Book Design & Typesetting: Chinook Design, Inc.

ISBN-13: 978-0-9819708-9-9

Printed in the United States of America

---

www.eWomenPublishingNetwork.com

Contents

CONTENTS

CONTENTS

CONTENTS

Introduction

Sandra Yancey

When we look at wildly successful people, it's easy to be dismissive, and make assumptions or projections, like: *they must have had it pretty easy* or *they must have had a backer* or *they must have been married to a spouse who funded them.* The list goes on and on.

One thing I've learned in my twelve years helping entrepreneurs around the world achieve, succeed and prosper, is that behind the reality of great successes are humbling moments of great despair.

It is the journey from despair to destiny that really shapes an entrepreneur. Entrepreneurs who experience disappointment and disillusionment, but never learn from them, continue to struggle and often never live their dream. Entrepreneurs who accept, feel and learn the realities of those tough moments; mourn their losses; seek meaning within them; and then build greatness *using them* are the ones who ultimately climb to the highest of heights.

Two years into my launch of eWomenNetwork, I was on the brink of bankruptcy. Coming off of a really successful corporate career, the dire situation really rattled me. I had never worked as hard in my life, for the least amount of money I had ever made. It really shook me to the core, and started playing with my mind and undermining my confidence. Raising two children under the age of eight, operating on four hours of sleep a night and taking on every job by myself, I wondered, *Can I really do this?* In addition to being on the brink of bankruptcy, I was on the brink of quitting.

One day my mother called to chat and asked me how things were going. I remember standing at the door, looking outside and thinking, *This day is so bright and beautiful, with such a gorgeous blue sky, yet inside I feel like I'm in the deepest storm ever.* I said to Mom, "I can't do this. I've got to find a job. I'll do eWomenNetwork on the side."

"Wait a minute," she said. "You're already working twenty hours a day. How are you going to get a job and expect this will work?"

Clouded by the fog of it all, I couldn't see her point of view. "Well, I really don't know, but I do know one thing, I can't pay my bills and I've got to quit," I replied.

---

*It is the journey from despair to destiny
that really shapes an entrepreneur.*

And then, like so many important times before, my mother's wisdom surfaced again and she asked me one poignant question: "How do you know you're not quitting five minutes before the miracle begins?"

I was quiet for a moment, and then said, "Well, I don't."

It was then that my mother really gave me the strength and power of outside forces. She said, "Well, honey, then you really can't quit. I'm not saying *don't* quit, but if you *do* quit, you have to *know.* You have to know that this is what you want and have to do. And you're not there yet. If you quit now, I promise you, you will spend the rest of your life wondering what might have been."

Her response really touched me, and I knew in my heart she was right, but the doubts lingered. "Then what do I do?" I said.

"I don't know," she replied. "But I know one thing: I raised a daughter smart enough to figure it out."

I was drowning, and with that simple statement, my mother reached in, pulled me out and saved me. She gave me the confidence to take that one next step. In that moment I realized that I didn't have to figure everything out right then; I just had to acknowledge that I didn't know, and then ask for help. After all, what was the worst thing that could happen?

You, too, may feel like you're drowning, wondering if you'll ever be able to make this dream of yours happen. You, too, may be tired, overworked, struggling to get by. You, too, may be ready

---

You are smart enough to figure it out, and you are not alone.

---

to quit. I may not know how you will pull it off, but I do know two things for sure: You are smart enough to figure it out, and you are not alone.

My vision for this book is rooted in a key principle of eWomen-Network: "Lift as You Climb." I believe if you really want to get somewhere in life, you have to be both a go-getter and a go-giver. A one-sided coin isn't worth anything; a silver dollar, a penny—the value is printed on both sides. Living a life of significance and self-actualization is about paying attention to both sides: being a go-getter, *and* a go-giver. As my wise mother used to say, "You've never really given in life until you've helped someone who can never pay you back."

With that in mind, I asked my girlfriends, bestselling authors, world-class speakers and thought leaders, Lisa Nichols, Marcia Wieder and Lisa Sasevich, and thirty-five other inspiring entrepreneurs to help me provide insights and inspiration for you and other visionaries on their way up. The co-authors in this book are people like you who had an idea, a dream, a goal, and when faced with challenges, they turned barriers into benchmarks, obstacles into opportunities, and setbacks into steppingstones—and succeeded, in spite of everything.

Together, it is our hope that *Succeeding In Spite Of Everything* is not only that ultimate healing medicine that gives you strength when you're feeling fatigued, a Band-Aid when you're feeling broken or sunlight when you're in darkness; but also that this is that book of wisdom you turn to on *good days* for further inspiration and ideas and insights.

And when you're in the catbird seat, I want you to remember where you came from. I want you to show up and assist someone who needs guidance and support, help someone else to feel less alone; I want you to lift as you climb. Never forget that you are but one resource away from the miracle beginning, and your own story... has yet to be written!

Play Full Out

Lisa Nichols

I'm nineteen, standing in front of my classmates, excited to deliver my first speech. My instructor has given me and my fellow students clear instructions: *Start with power. Capture the attention of your audience. Hold their attention. Make eye contact. Test the waters. Close with power.*

I go over his instructions and all of my notes; I know I'm about to deliver a powerful speech. I begin: "Why? Why did he touch me? Why did he put his hands on my body inappropriately? I have no idea. He's supposed to be my babysitter…"

My audience is captivated; everyone holds their breath. I can't tell whether the room is excited by me, or just mortified by my comments. Whatever it is, it's good; I am on fire! When the speech is over, I am elated. *I did it,* I think. *I shocked them. I was edgy. I maintained eye contact…*

My stomach bubbles with excitement. I feel alive, and I know I will never be the same.

I was born to take words and massage them, highlight them, give bold meaning to them, speak them at the top of my voice or whisper them in a breath. I was born to communicate with words. As I grew up, speaking and leading my peers felt effortless. I felt it in middle school and in high school. Seeing my fellow students get excited with me, *because of me,* felt amazing. I remember saying,

"I know I will have a role in the world that requires speaking and leadership," but I had no idea what that job would be.

Born and raised in South Central Los Angeles, the only speakers I ever saw were preachers, and I didn't want to become a preacher. Though they inspired me, and I loved the feeling their speeches gave me, their messages of God's love also seemed to come with messages of fire and brimstone, and that didn't appeal to me. Motivational speakers like Les Brown and Tony Robbins hadn't made it to my community yet, so I had no idea there were other options... until my freshman year in college.

When I saw the speaking class in my course catalog, I was beyond excited. *Oh my God! I have no idea what I'm going to do with this, but I want to take this class!* I almost felt guilty taking the class for a grade; though I didn't think it would be an easy A, because of my natural ability I knew it would be a *delicious* A.

My audience is captivated;
everyone holds their breath.

In the class I learn that speaking could be a profession, and I am stunned. *There are people who do this nine to five, five days a week?* It feels as if I've discovered uranium!

Now, standing before my classmates, their eyes as big as saucers, I know I've moved them. *This is it. This is what I am meant to do.* As I take my seat, my heart beats fast and I imagine a lifetime of motivating the masses with my voice, my words, my stories, my light.

I go on to deliver four more speeches, just like the first. I choose the topics no one else wants to talk about, topics that matter to me: racism in America, homeless children, sexual abuse. With every speech, I am lit up from the inside; I am in my element.

When the class comes to an end, I'm confident I will get a strong grade. The professor calls me up to his desk, looks at me, and turns the grade book around to show me my mark, a D-minus. My whole body goes numb, as if time has stopped. *D-minus? I followed the guidelines. I delivered five powerful speeches on subjects that matter to the world. I know my words touched hearts and minds. What happened?*

My professor's next comment shakes me out of my stunned state. "Bad just got worse. Miss Nichols, it's my recommendation that you never speak in public. I recommend you get a desk job."

I walk away baffled, too confused to focus on my hurt. I'm confident in my gift of charismatic speaking; nothing makes sense. *I don't understand—I followed the guidelines, I picked bold topics, I maintained eye contact, I used visual aids. How did I get a D-minus? Why would he say I should never speak in public?*

"Miss Nichols, it's my recommendation that you never speak in public. I recommend you get a desk job."

That same year, I took an English class. At the time, my nickname would have been "run-on-sentence Mama," which is how I speak. A few weeks before I received my D-minus in speech, I learned that I failed English. *Failed.* Because I had struggled in the class, I was expecting a low grade, but I didn't expect to actually fail the class.

Worse, in front of the classroom my teacher said, "Lisa, you have to be the weakest writer I've ever met in my entire life."

After her comment, I leaned on the fact that I was a good speaker. A *great* speaker. But now, in my speech class, I've been told I'm never to speak in public and I'm really confused. *I shouldn't write and I shouldn't speak?* I can feel the fire in me die down to slow-burning embers, as my vision for my future, so full of light and hope just moments before, wilts in the face of authoritative criticism. *They're the experts. They must know something I don't know, and what they know is I am not a speaker and I am not a writer.*

Even though I respect their opinion and opt to follow their advice, something in my body doesn't agree with the direction they have set for me or the limitations they have placed on my heart. I know I am supposed to speak in front of millions. I feel it. I hear the call. I see it. *I know.* But I'm not strong enough, mature enough or astute enough either to push back or to find a way to push forward in spite of them.

Within a year I am kicked out of college because my family doesn't have the finances to pay my tuition. I go back to South Central L.A. and become a community advocate.

When asked why I choose this path, I say, "Being an advocate is like being a cheerleader. I can do that. I can be a cheerleader for the people."

I sound confident in my decision, but inside I know the path I walk is littered with insecurity; the path I walk is the one laid out for me by my professors. *I'm not supposed to write, or hold the*

"God, call me back later; I'm inspiring L.A."

---

microphone too long, but I can inspire these people. I can fight for their rights, for funds to make their lives better. That I can do.

Though my belly keeps telling me my purpose is motivating the masses, I keep arguing with my knowing, with the spirit inside of me. *Didn't you hear what the teacher said? He said you should never speak in public.* I argue so vehemently that in my early twenties, I take an accounting course and get a job in the accounts receivable department of a medium-sized company. *He said, "I recommend you get a desk job."* I am terrible at this job! The worst thing you can do is make someone who doesn't believe in forcing people to do things force people to pay bills with money they say they don't have.

One day, my supervisor calls me into her office and says, "Lisa, what do you want to be?"

Thinking she is testing my loyalty, I reply, "I want to be the manager of the collections department!"

She cringes and says, "No. You can't want to be manager of collections because you don't do it very well."

In that moment, I realize this isn't going to be a meeting to acknowledge the good work I am doing; this is a meeting that could end drastically. My face falls, and I blurt out, "Oh, my God, are you firing me?"

My supervisor says, "Lisa, you are one of the nicest people I've ever met. You're kind and loving, but you don't make people pay their accounts. I'm not firing you; I'm releasing you to go find your dream."

Soon after being fired, I realized that I had minimized my possibilities. I had said, "I can do L.A. I can go into low-income neighborhoods and shake the cage and get funds for them, play big in my small little world. In L.A., I can be the bomb-dot-com."

But God wasn't having it. He would call me and say, "I need you to inspire the world."

And I would say, "God, call me back later; I'm inspiring L.A."

God would call me back, like a stalker! It was as if he put his finger on the redial button and called me twenty seconds later. "Lisa, I need you to inspire the world."

And I would say, "Didn't I just tell you I could do L.A.?"

Now I knew I had been playing it safe and it was time to answer the call. When you are called to use your voice in a mighty way, don't rest until you do exactly that. Overcome any negative chatter; silence the consultant, the committee, the *authorities,* the entire

---

Now I knew I had been playing it safe
and it was time to answer the call.

Verizon network in your mind. Because when you are designed to deliver a message to the world, you will not have peace of mind until you do. Whether you spend eighteen days, eighteen months, or eighteen years like me trying to avoid that calling, God will keep calling you back until you take his call and say, "Yes!"

I spend my days now working with people who are assigned to play big in the world, and realize they are late for work. They were called a long time ago, and like me, they spent way too many years trying to convince the universe and themselves that they are only supposed to play out a portion of their greatness. Today, I teach them how to live in transparency and free others to do the same, how to serve and not sell, how to deliver high impact on their worst days.

Eighteen years after my professors told me not to speak or write, thirteen years after I was fired to go find my dream, I'm speaking at an eWomenNetwork conference. Standing in the wings while my intro video rolls—me with Oprah, with Larry King, talking about *The Secret,* about my books, about inspiring millions—I notice a woman crying in the audience. I think, *Normally I make them cry toward the middle or the end. This woman is crying, and I haven't even started yet*!

I go on and do my thing, and after my keynote speech I stand in line to greet and hug the 285 women who waited to see me. I look over and see the same woman standing off to the side, still bawling her eyes out.

Finally, I excuse myself from the line, walk up to her and say, "Excuse me ma'am, you've been crying since I got on stage, and you're *still* crying. Why are you crying so much?"

She looks at me and chokes out, "Because I fired you thirteen years ago!"

I scream to everyone in the line, "Oh my God! It's my supervisor, the one who fired me because I really sucked at accounting!"

The people in line start crying; I turn to the woman and say, "Thank you for firing me."

She smiles then, because her tears are joyful tears. We hold each other, both of us bawling now, and I offer a silent prayer of thanks. Then she steps back a little, takes my hands in her own and says, "Look at you, look at your gift. You found your dream."

And though I didn't say it at the time I thought, *No, I found it a long time ago. It just took me eighteen years to get it back.*

LISA NICHOLS

New York Times *bestselling author Lisa Nichols has reached millions around the world with her message of empowerment, service, excellence and gratitude. Founder of Motivating the Masses and CEO of Motivating Teen Spirit, LLC, Lisa is a charismatic teacher, speaker and transformational coach. She appeared in the self-development phenomenon* The Secret *and on* The Oprah Winfrey Show *and* Larry King Live. *The co-author of the bestselling books* Chicken Soup for the African American's Soul, Chicken Soup for the African American Woman's Soul, Living Proof *and* Unbreakable Spirit, *her book* No Matter What! *hit six bestseller lists including the* New York Times, *and has been translated into twenty-eight languages.*

Lisa has been honored with many awards for her empowering work, including the Humanitarian Award from South Africa. In keeping with her commitment to help people who have a global assignment to use their voice to motivate, educate, activate, inspire and transform, Lisa developed Powerhouse Speakers, her first training program that shares her secrets and techniques for becoming a dynamic, transformational speaker. Connect with Lisa at www.Lisa-Nichols.com.

What If?

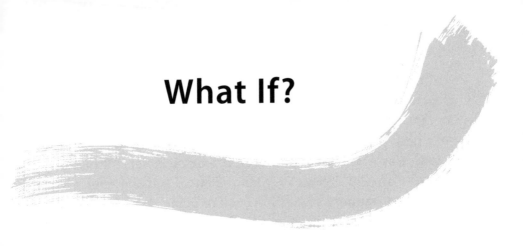

Marcia Wieder

People often say to me, "I'd go for my dreams if I only had enough money."

So, I typically ask, "How much money do you need?"

The most common answer I receive is, "I don't know, but I know I don't have enough."

More often than not, we fail ourselves before life can fail us. We kill or compromise our dreams before we ever explore the possibilities, projecting our fears and doubts onto the dream. We do this with three simple words: "But what if… ?"

"But what if I fail? But what if I make the wrong choices? But what if really don't have enough talent, education, support, money, time to pull this off?"

Our attitudes and beliefs determine our thoughts and feelings, and from that we make choices and decisions. If your dream is to start your own business, and your core belief about that is, "I don't really know what I'm doing," you'll start in with the "But what ifs." From that, your logical choice and decision would probably be to forget about the dream. If, on the other hand, your core foundational belief is, "I believe in myself," your thoughts and feelings might be, "This is something that matters to me." Building on those thoughts and feelings, your logical choice and decision would be to go for it.

Attitudes and beliefs are never neutral; they either move us forward or hold us back. I think we're all pretty aware of that by now. But what so many of us have forgotten is: We can choose what we believe. Can you believe in something, not because there are promises, assurances or guarantees, but simply because it matters to you? Can you believe in your dream of starting your own business, or writing a bestselling book or living abroad because it matters to you—and then prove it matters to you by actually doing something about it?

Years ago, I bought an expensive house in Northern California with a million-dollar view of the Golden Gate Bridge. It was a funky little half-renovated cottage, and I figured I'd make it mine and then grow old there. When I began to put in a new bathroom, the contractor found a massive crack in a load-bearing wall. I soon

> *Our attitudes and beliefs determine*
> *our thoughts and feelings.*

discovered the previous owner had put in a false floor to cover up the fact that the house had slipped eight inches on the foundation. When I was told, "The house has to come down," I was devastated. I thought, *My life savings are in this house; my dreams are in this house; my future is in this house. What am I going to do?*

For years, my life was consumed with righting this wrong. I was up to my neck in lawsuits—with the sellers, the realtors, the inspector who told me I was buying a solid home—and living in a half-gutted, and therefore mildewing, house while working my butt off to pay the legal fees. I had gained thirty pounds, gone into early menopause and felt as though I was carrying around a deep dark secret: I never wanted anyone to know that "America's Dream Coach" was living through this hellish nightmare.

Four years and four-hundred-thousand dollars later, I was done. I told my attorney, "Get me in front of a judge."

When the judge said, "I'm sorry to tell you this, but the law doesn't necessarily protect the innocent," my heart dropped to my stomach. He went on to say, "The land you're living on is worth more than the house. You could spend years of your life and thousands of dollars, and in the end, you could lose."

That day I fired my attorney and went looking for another house. During the four years of hell I had hired an architect to design a Mediterranean-style villa, assuming I would rebuild once I was permitted to tear down the house I had come to call "the

---

When I was told, "The house has to come down," I was devastated.

---

dump." So, when I found a Mediterranean-style villa, I knew it was my house. I could see the Christmas tree in the foyer and friends laughing in the kitchen. There was only one problem. Okay, *two* problems. The mortgage for the villa was double my current mortgage, and I would be making mortgage payments on the dump for the foreseeable future. Not surprisingly, everyone told me not to buy the new house.

This is when I came up with "The Myth of Prerequisites," that A doesn't necessarily have to come before B. If you're creative, you can think outside of the box.

When I called my financial planner, he said, "I have good news and bad news. The good news is that because you worked your butt off these past few years, you can afford the down payment." When I asked him to give me the bad news, he said, "You can't afford two mortgages."

When I hung up I had a "come to Jesus" moment. *Marcia, you teach people not to look in their checkbooks to see if their dream is a good idea. You stand for: Don't let doubt and fear be obstacles when something really matters to you. If you don't take this leap of faith and go for your dream home, you'll be a hypocrite and your career as a speaker, author and teacher will be over.*

I took a leap of faith and bought that very expensive Mediterranean-style dream home. Very soon, I found myself camped out on an air mattress with a bottle of Veuve Clicquot champagne. When the sun rose, the answer came to me. *I know who's going to buy the dump!*

I called the builder of my new home and asked him to meet me at the old property. When he arrived, I showed him the plans I had had drawn up for the Mediterranean-style villa I had hoped to build there. I said, "Can't you picture the kitchen window here? And the upstairs looking out to the bridge?"

He said, "Yes, I can," and, with the money he paid me for the lot, I was able to pay down the mortgage on my dream palace, and live in my new home for the same amount of money I had been paying to live in the dump.

When I took that leap of faith, believing in my vision for my home and my life, new resources and new perspectives showed up that would not have shown up when I was in the "figuring it out" stage. Had I not bought the house, the builder would not have been a prospect for buying the dump.

What I teach is, and how it changed me was, there is a level of deep faith that, when tapped into, allows us to dream bigger dreams, take bigger risks and act on what's important to us, even without evidence that this is a good idea or that this is the right time to pursue it.

Part of our mission at Dream University is to change the way people think about, speak about and act upon their dreams. In school, we learn the A-B-Cs. At Dream University, we teach the C-B-As: C—get clear about what you do and don't want, B—believe in yourself (which is a choice), and A—demonstrate that you do believe in yourself, that you are more committed to your dream than you are to doubt, fear or reality, by taking action on your dream.

Many of us have forgotten that we can choose what we believe. The number-one way we sabotage our dreams is by projecting our thoughts and fears onto them, the "But what ifs." If you haven't dealt with your own doubts, and you meet another doubter on the road, their doubt will magnify yours. But, if you've dealt with your doubt, and then you meet a doubter on the road, your contrast with their doubt actually becomes an opportunity to deepen your commitment to your dream.

Develop the ability to talk to anyone, at any time, in any place about your dream; you'll be well on your way to the short cut. In order to master manifestation, you must master the skill of enrollment, or inspiring other people to join you, help you or invest in you. I so believed in my dream home that I had no doubt it would work, and therefore was able to enroll the builder in helping me make it happen. The obstacle called "I don't have enough money" disappears when you master the ability to talk to anyone, anytime about your dreams.

I've seen people go further with passion and commitment than with skill and gobs of money. A big mistake I see people make over

---

*The only thing that quells the voice
of the doubter is action.*

---

and over again is going to strategy too soon. I encourage you to hang out longer in the "what if" instead of the "but what if?" What if you had all of the time and money you need? What if your family supported you without question? What if you truly believed you could not fail?

What if?

Open up to the greater dream and possibility, and then deal with the C-B-As. Get clear about your dream, then look at your doubts, fears and limitations; create a foundational belief (*I will live in my dream home*) that will support you in being more committed to your dream; and then take action. The only thing that quells the voice of the doubter is action.

The greatest thing you can do to make your dreams come true is pump your integrity muscle, where you keep your agreements with yourself, with others and, on a spiritual level, with God.

To me, success is getting to your own ideal version of happiness, and whatever internal (beliefs and doubts) or external (circumstances beyond your control) barriers are holding you back, you can become successful. Trust the process of getting clear about who you are, what you want and how you want your life to be And then have the clarity, the courage and the confidence to be able to create a life that is really successful on your own terms, because success is living the highest, best version of yourself every day.

All good things come from this place, a place where external realities and perceived obstacles are merely speed bumps on the road to your dreams.

Dream University's CEO/founder Marcia Wieder is committed to helping one-million dreams come true over the next year. The author of fourteen books, she has appeared on Oprah *and* The Today Show *and was featured on the PBS-TV program* Making Your Dreams Come True. *As a columnist for the* San Francisco Chronicle, *Marcia urged readers to take "The Great Dream Challenge." She is a member of the Transformational Leadership Council with Jack Canfield and John Gray. As past president of the National Association of Women Business Owners, she assisted three U.S. presidents and now serves on the advisory board for the Make-A-Wish Foundation. To connect with Marcia and receive three of her powerful eBooks, please go to www. DreamUniversity.com/gift.*

Listen. Act. Trust.

Lisa Sasevich

Has the Universe ever given you a gentle tap? A little signal, something you wouldn't think of yourself? I call these taps from intuition, from Spirit, from Source, inspiration.

All too often, when we have those little inspired thoughts, like: *I should give to this person; I should help with that; I should step back here; I should step forward over there,* we talk ourselves out of them. We're inspired in the moment, but then we think about it too long. We say: *That's a crazy idea; That doesn't make sense. That's inconvenient. That would be hard. That's expensive.* That is our smaller self—our head, our brain, our mentality—talking our higher self—our heart, our wisdom, our connection to Source— out of an inner knowing that we experienced.

The more you keep taking action on those inspirations without second guessing, without a lot of analysis-paralysis, the more you're going to experience moving forward with your life and encounter little miracles you would never have dreamt of. And, if you don't pay attention to the little tap, sometimes the Universe hits you with a two-by-four.

My own whack with a two-by-four came when I was let go from a company for which I was one of the top sellers. I thought I'd be working with that company forever, because I really loved their work, and I was good at it. After that "gentle tap," I started questioning what am I here for; what is the blessing, the gift, I have to share? I call this "getting on your dime." Think about Oprah, doing what she was made to do. Think of Tony Robbins, doing his blessing for thirty-five years or so. They tapped into their intuitions, and in doing so, tapped into their million-dollar value.

Often our million-dollar value is so close to us that we can't see it. It's what everybody sees as our gift, but we're blind to it. It's that particular thing we do that comes easily for us, so we don't think of it as having a million-dollar value, but to everyone else, it's astonishing. In my case, it's the ability to craft irresistible offers and inspire people to invest in themselves and to teach heart-centered entrepreneurs how to do the same. That's my gift.

After I was let go, I started signing up for a lot of free trainings and entry-level programs, ever trying to gain insight, better myself and learn new strategies. Until I got hit by the two-by-four, I had resisted making a deeper investment in myself. Finally, I got hungry

If you don't pay attention to the little tap, sometimes the Universe hits you with a two-by-four.

enough for a breakthrough that I was inspired to dig deep and take a risk, to make a significant financial investment in myself and my future. It was time to get out there with my own expertise, rather than just contribute to other people's companies.

The first big investment I made was in a training course that would teach me how to get my gifts out online. It was an offer over the Internet, and it cost three-thousand dollars, which, even with the six-payments plan, was way more money than I had lying around.

My then-husband was in medical school, and we had a one-year-old and a three-year-old. It wasn't just the money. I was running everything and taking care of the kids, as well as providing a lot of the financial support. So, it was a huge leap. But, that course kept showing up in my inbox and glaring at me more than all the other emails. I resisted as long as I could until I shot up out of bed one night saying, "I just have to do this."

So, I followed the inspiration with action and signed up for the course. The course wasn't going to begin for another six months, but I'd made that commitment. I said, "Hey, I'm going to get my blessing out there; I'm going to invest in learning how to get out there." That commitment, that investment, lit a fire under me. I got

---

Often our million-dollar value is so close to us that we can't see it.

---

serious, and I carved out time and I did the work. It was almost as though I told the Universe, "I believe in myself," and it resonated out into the world, and guess what, the people I spoke to picked it up, and they believed in what I could offer them too.

I listened, I acted and I trusted. And, before the course began, I got the courage, the ovaries, to make a $3,000 offer to my clients. I'd never offered anything over $250 before, so it was a big leap. Eight people took advantage of my offer, and this really gave me some courage. Now, I had money to pay off the course that still hadn't begun. I thought, *What's another tool I can use in my business, so I can invest some of this money back into myself? Doing that seems to work for me.* I invested in another course, one that cost $7500. And, within three weeks I was selling my own new program for guess how much? Yes… $7500. I sold it to six of the seven people that I first talked to. I wasn't through with the course yet, and I hadn't even started the first one.

There's something important about investing in yourself. It lights a fire under you, more than most other things can do. More than dreaming about it, more than affirmations, more than writing down goals. There's something about putting your money where your mouth is.

My own personal highest values are peace, faith and abundance. If I keep those at the forefront of my mind when I'm making decisions, then I experience being successful as a person.

For instance, I was in really uncomfortable circumstances after my father passed away and the family started getting into a lot of turmoil about his estate that was just heartbreaking. I got some great advice from my colleague and friend Alexis Neely, who said, "Well, what are your highest values? Why don't you put those at the forefront and then make a decision based on that?" And based on my commitment to being peaceful, faithful and abundant, I chose to let go and remove myself from all the conflict.

Sometimes we listen to the little signals from the Universe; we do that crazy thing that doesn't make much sense to us. Then we start second-guessing and we torture ourselves. Peace falls away.

There's something about putting
your money where your mouth is.

Listen. Act. Trust. Trust the action you took. When you take an action—such as when you make a big investment in yourself, or you help someone in a big way or you, as I shared earlier about my father's estate, choose to step back—trust the action you took, that you took it based on an inspiration, a tap from Source.

Every single one of us is born with a unique blessing, a unique gift. For example, there might be fifty different people who do belief-change work. Every one of them has a particular angle, a particular gift, a particular flavor that they bring to their work. You could line all of them up in a row, and a client would know specifically who she is supposed to work with. Now obviously, part of the task with marketing is to articulate that. In our programs, we help entrepreneurs articulate their gift—what is their offer, the unique outcome that they provide, distinct from everyone else?

When you know your highest values and you operate congruently with them, that will call you to be the person you want to be. When you get wins, material and financial, that are not consistent with your values, then you don't feel successful. You're left feeling empty. But, when you're operating from your highest values that are calling you to be the person you strive to be, you stretch to be, then when you experience wins, they feel like success because they're consistent with who you are.

Aligning your million-dollar value with your highest values is the key. In my new book, *The Live Sassy Formula,* we help readers clarify their "Sassy Mission." Within that, the concept of "getting on your dime" is birthed. Your dime is what you were made to do, that thing you simply can't NOT do. This is your million-dollar value. In the book, we outline many ways to get closer to your dime, but one of my favorites is to identify what you think it *might* be, and then get out into the world and speak about it. It's amazing how quickly a live audience helps you see what they most want from you. That instant feedback is gold.

It doesn't have to take a near-death experience, or a tragedy, or even a "two-by-four" to make us realize that life is not a dress rehearsal.

Start by listening to those little taps, take inspired action and then trust the action you took.

LISTEN. ACT. TRUST.

Lisa Sasevich is a bestselling author and world-renowned speaker and trainer. Known as "The Queen of Sales Conversion," she teaches experts who are making a difference how to get their message out and enjoy massive results, without being "sales-y." After twenty-five years of winning top sales awards and training senior executives at companies like Pfizer and Hewlett-Packard, Lisa left corporate America and put her skills to the test as an entrepreneur. In just a few short years she created a multi-million-dollar home-based business with two toddlers in tow and her husband in medical school. Recognized as a sales expert by Success Magazine, *Lisa was honored as one of America's Top Women Mentoring Leaders by* WoW Magazine. *She is the author of the bestselling book,* The Live Sassy Formula: Make Big Money and a Big Difference Doing What You Love! *Connect with Lisa at www.LisaSasevich.com.*

Put Yourself in My Place

Venus Opal Reese, PhD

Put yourself in my place.

You are sixteen, living on the streets of Baltimore. Around you are drugs, violence, police and prostitution. You can predict your future: welfare, trickin', addiction and death. You sit on your street corner, steeped in urine and beer, and ask yourself, *How did I get here?* You answer: *Momma.*

Put yourself in my place.

Rewind to a younger you, maybe eleven or twelve, and you have a brand new Jheri Curl. A Jheri Curl is an 80s hair style—think Eddie Murphy's movie, *Coming to America.* It's like a wet, curly perm for black people. To a little black girl, a Jheri Curl means you are beautiful.

You walk into the house. It is way too quiet, way too still. Momma's angry again. You don't know why, but you know it is directed at you. Momma is what black people from the South call a "Georgia Peach." Pecan-brown skin, five-foot-three, Coke-bottle frame with a wit—and temper—as quick as lightning and as deadly. Unpredictable and dangerous. She could strike at any time.

"Oh well. Lookie here. Got your hair did, huh. Oh, you think you cute now, huh? You think you grown."

You hold your breath. You say nothing. You don't know where this is going, but you don't want to give her any reason to strike.

"Whatchu lookin' at? Get you ass up the stairs!" Momma pushes you up the stairs and shoves you down on the bed.

You say nothing.

"You move, your ass is grass!" Momma leaves the bedroom.

You hold your breath, obedient and terrified.

Momma marches back into the room. She has scissors. She grasps a fistful of your long, damp curls and jerks your head back. It hurts. Snap. Snap. Your hair begins to fall. Down your arms. Into your lap. Onto the bed.

You say nothing.

"Now no one will look at you."

Clumps of damp curls lie all around you. You touch your head. The cut is uneven and you have blood on your scalp where hair used to be. The air stings as it hits the bloody bald spots. You say nothing. In that moment, you decide some things. Big things.

---

*Unpredictable and dangerous. She
could strike at any time.*

Things that will have you living hand to mouth in four brief years. You decide you are stupid (because you didn't move); you decide you are ugly (because Momma said no one will look at you); and you decide life is dangerous—so you are on your own. So you take to the streets.

Put yourself in my place.

Now you are on your corner, Monument and Federal Street, right around the corner from Johns Hopkins University. Reeking of piss and Budweiser, you pray, "God, please help me get out."

It's that time of the month and you don't have protection. So you use toilet paper. You come to school and your aroma precedes you.

"Damn, you stink!" One of the high school bullies pinches his nose while he points at you in the hall.

The in-crowd laugh and make faces; you hold your head down trying to find the door to sixth period math class without meeting any eyes. The teachers monitoring the hall turn their heads, pretending they don't see your tattered coat, your threadbare pants, your sockless feet in shoes with holes.

You sit in the back of Mrs. Francis's classroom in the last row, in the farthest corner, praying no one notices you. Mrs. Francis is no joke. The kids are scared of her because she don't take no mess. She is four–foot-ten, light brown skin, pretty, long black hair, heavyset, with an attitude. When the kids start to whisper

---

This begins your trust relationship with
Mrs. Francis. It all happens in the unsaid.

---

and point at you, Mrs. Francis quickly interjects, "Uh, do you want a zero? No? Then I suggest you face the front of the room, do those math problems and stop all that snickering. If not, then take your zero and get out of my class!" No more snickering from the students. A wave of relief and shame washes over you at her protectiveness.

After class, Mrs. Francis helps you get cleaned up, takes you for something to eat and drops you off at the corner of Monument and Federal. You say nothing and Mrs. Francis doesn't ask any questions. You keep your dignity. This begins your trust relationship with Mrs. Francis. It all happens in the unsaid.

You start to hang out after school to wipe down Mrs. Francis's blackboards. She takes you to get food and leaves things for you on your chair in the back of her math class: a book one week, a pair of thick socks the next.

You stopped talking months ago. But you show your appreciation by taking out the trash, helping her put up her bulletin boards and leaving books on her desk.

One day, you are reading a book in the back of math class. Mrs. Francis marches to the your desk and says with conviction and authority, "If you are not going to talk, then write!" She shoves a pencil and a pad in your hand. She marches back to the front of the room and acts like nothing happened.

You figure you don't want to piss her off—and lose out on free food—so you should do what she says. You write down your thoughts. Your thoughts come out as poetry. You leave the pad on her desk and rush out.

Mrs. Francis reads your words, types them up and mails them to the NAACP-ACTSO Writing Competition and you win.

Winning the competition was surreal. But winning wasn't what altered the course of my life. It was something much more profound.

Someone had cared enough about me to read my words. The closest analogy I can think of is the water pump scene from Helen

---

*Winning wasn't what altered
the course of my life.*

Keller's story, *The Miracle Worker*. When Helen's teacher, Anne Sullivan, kept repeating "w-a-t-e-r" as Helen felt the invisible force flowing over her hand, in the moment she connected that force with the word *water* she became a sentient being. She was pulled out of the darkness of deafness and blindness. Consciousness was born.

Mrs. Francis was a stranger, a regular ol' inner city high school teach who gave me the tools to have a voice (pencil and pad), turned herself into a resource (a math teacher who looked for that poetry contest so I would have a different experience of myself) and poured love on me.

When I fully comprehended what Mrs. Francis had done for me, I became a social being. I realized for the first time in my life that I mattered. I had intrinsic worth that I did not—could not— earn or pay for. Mrs. Francis had given it all to me for free. I had a new thought: *Mrs. Francis sees me differently than I see me. I see me as worthless—with all the evidence to prove it. Mrs. Francis sees me as someone worth somethin'. If I saw me the way Mrs. Francis sees me, maybe I could do somethin' with my life.*

28

That one thought changed everything. I started to act like someone who sees herself as somebody that matters. I got two part-time jobs—scrubbing floors and selling shoes—that paid for new clothes. I found safe places to stay for a week or two at a time. I copied people who looked like they had it together—how they stood, talked, laughed. Our sense of self determines our destiny, and I was re-shaping mine.

> *Our sense of self determines our destiny, and I was re-shaping mine.*

Fourteen years later, I am set to graduate with a second master's degree and a PhD from Stanford University. It matters to put myself in Momma's shoes: A seventeen-year-old who found her mother dead; a woman violated and beat by the men who said they loved her; a mother who lost her firstborn to heroin laced with embalming fluid.

When I can put myself in her place, I call. "Momma, I am so sorry. You didn't take your love away from me. I took my love away from you. Will you forgive me?"

"You were a hard child to raise."

"I know, Momma—"

"No, you don't know—"

"You're right, I don't know. I don't."

Then she proceeds to tell me everything I ever did wrong, and I am happy. I can hear what she is not saying. Behind all the blame, beyond all the finger-pointing, beneath all the accusations, I hear heart. I sense her reaching across emotional gulfs generations deep in the only language she has. I hear her saying I love you.

"I love you, Momma. Will you come to graduation? I want you there." I hold my breath. Long pause.

"Yes."

Exhale. Cry. Give thanks. Both Momma and Mrs. Francis walked me across stage to get my degree.

From the streets of Baltimore to the hallowed halls of Stanford—it might look as though the victory was the degrees. It wasn't. Graduation was simply the stage I used to say thank you to the two most important women in my life: the woman who gave me life and the woman who saved my life.

Now my entire life is dedicated to helping women know they matter. When you know you matter, when you can see yourself with new eyes and take actions consistent with who you say you are *for yourself* instead of what history says, or experience tells you, or even what your momma said, you create your destiny. You live, love and leverage your intrinsic worth in the world. You defy the impossible.

Venus Opal Reese, MA, PhD, is an inspirational speaker, executive mentor, and award-winning theatre artist. She has consulted for O The Oprah Magazine, *and has been featured on ABC News, CBS News, PBS, and the Associated Press and in* Glamour *and* Diversity Inc. *Her award-nominated solo performance work was produced Off-Broadway, and she has presented at the Sorbonne. She is proud to be a former Coast Guard Reservist.*

Dr. Venus is the founder and CEO of Defy Impossible, Inc., a successful personal and professional development company based in the Dallas, Texas area. Her keynotes, programs, trainings, services and systems are based on over twenty years of research, teaching, personal experience and multiple branches of theoretical and philosophical training. She delivers authentic, high-impact, customized success strategies and keynotes for purpose-driven CEOs, executives and entrepreneurs. Her strategies, systems and services unleash an individual's heart-center to help her make big money and make a big difference while being profoundly respected and fulfilled.

Dr. Venus has written many popular and scholarly articles and essays about identity, effectiveness and leadership. She has presented to organizations such as the U.S. Department of Social Security, the U.S. Department for Homeland Security and the Dallas-Fort Worth International Airport, as well as Harvard, Yale, Northwestern, MIT and Stanford. Unanimously selected as one of the most impactful and important "must see" presenters of today by eWomenNetwork, she is a member of the National Speakers Association, the International Federation for Professional Speakers and WBENC, and is an elected board member of WordSpace, a nonprofit literary arts organization. Connect with Dr. Venus at www.DefyImpossible.com and www.DrVenusOpalReese.com.

Soaring Further

Elizabeth McCormick

Have you ever seen something before it happened and just knew it was meant to be?

From the very first moment I watched the pilots from behind the fence along the Fort Polk flight line, I knew I would fly too. The vision was so clear—so much more powerful than a daydream. I saw myself on the other side of the fence, wearing my green flight suit and helmet and standing next to the helicopters. I'd never even considered flying before. I didn't know how, but I knew now with my whole being that I was going to make it happen.

I learned a lot about determination and vision from my parents, who both went to college for the first time while working full-time and raising three kids. As eldest, I took on plenty of responsibility.

I went to college on a scholarship. In my last year, I met the man I affectionately call "the starter husband." He was going into the military. We fell in love and got married, and I moved to Fort Polk, Louisiana where he was stationed; but, I couldn't find a job. Nobody local would hire a military wife who would be leaving in two or three years. And, in 1993 we were in the midst of a recession, and there was a hiring freeze on base. After five years in college, graduating magna cum laude, the only job I could find was in a pizza joint. I knew I was meant to do more with my life—I just didn't know what.

One day I looked at my starter husband and thought, *If he can be in the Army, I can do it too.* With my degree, I could enter as a lieutenant on the RLO (Real Life Officer) track. I talked to the RLOs in my husband's unit, and they all advised, "Do you have good eyesight? Are you really healthy? Go with Warrant Officer flight training." *Fly?* I had never even thought about it. The RLOs hooked me up with some people they knew out at the flight line, and I went there to talk with the pilots.

So, I had already done all this research—and then gone to the flight line and had my vision—when I walked into the Army recruiter's office and said, "I want to fly. I want to sign up for the Warrant Officer Flight Training Program."

I knew I was meant to do more with my life—I just didn't know what.

The recruiter looked at me like I was crazy, and said, "You can't do that."

I swallowed the lump in my throat and said, "Yes, I can."

"But—but—but—" he sputtered, "you need a degree!"

"I have it," I replied.

"You need *leadership experience,*" he said.

"I have it," I said, and rattled off all my college experience.

"You need a perfect physical with perfect eyesight."

"I have it," I said firmly.

Exasperated, he paused. Then he began, "I don't know how...."

I broke in, "Then, we'll learn together."

In the beginning, it had nothing to do with patriotism; I needed a job. But, the bottom line was, it was cool. If I was going to do something, I was going to do something that kicked ass. Why NOT? So confident was I that when I was sent to Basic Training, I brought along everything I would need for Basic *plus* the Warrant Officer Candidate School (WOCS). On the first real day of Basic, when the drill sergeants made all of us trainees dump everything we brought with us onto our bunks, Drill Sergeant Gil found my

Army Officer Guide Book. "OH! You think you're going to be an officer when you haven't even made it through Basic Training yet?" *Well—yeah!* I thought. I'd seen that vision, and I had confidence it would be real.

I graduated second in my Basic Training class, and was the first female to graduate at the top of my WOCS class while leading as Candidate Staff. The very first phase of flight school after WOCS is medical and aerodynamics—the basics. But then you're in a helicopter immediately after that. I'd always excelled academically, but now I had to learn what an engine was. I didn't know how to read a map. It was a struggle. But, it was the physicality of flying that was hardest. Flying a helicopter is *not* like flying a plane and not even close to driving a car or anything else I had ever experienced.

Each foot operates independently on the pedals. Your right hand is on the cyclic, and not only are you controlling the bird with your cyclic, you're also controlling the microphone with a finger trigger and keeping your left hand on the collective. You're on the radio; you're talking on a lip microphone with air traffic

---

I couldn't relax enough to do it with my instructor pilot, Buck, screaming at me.

---

control; you're keeping an eye on the map strapped to your knee; and you're constantly scanning for obstacles. It's multitasking on anabolic steroids—*then add hovering!* I couldn't hover. It's not that I couldn't, actually; I couldn't relax enough to do it with my instructor pilot, Buck, screaming at me.

In training, the saying is, "Gently, gently as you go. A soft touch is best." In fact, once you're trained, you can control the direction of a helicopter with one finger on the cyclic. But, not when you're first starting. Every day I'd go to the flight line in Fort Rucker, Alabama and mentally prepare to be yelled at. As soon as my hands touched the bird's controls, Buck's berating began. And my doubts would creep in: *What was I thinking?* There I was, trying to fly a multimillion-dollar UH-1H Huey while this guy made every minute in the cockpit a living hell. He didn't agree with women flying helicopters, but he couldn't fail me only because of that. He could sure scream at me while I flew, though, and try to make me fail.

I'd say to myself, *I'm not going to let it get to me; I'm not going to let it get to me.* But, despite my will, my hand would tense, the movement would translate to the cyclic, and the helicopter would start swinging like a pendulum. A veer to the right, and I'd clench and overcorrect to the left, the bird swinging dangerously back and forth. And the whole time Buck yelled, "IT'S SO EASY! WHY CAN'T YOU DO THIS? WHAT MAKES YOU THINK YOU ARE GOOD ENOUGH TO FLY?" He never yelled at my stick buddy, Ryan. But, at the end my turn at the controls, I could hear Buck thinking triumphantly, "FAIL!"

Ryan, on the other hand, totally got it. We hovered and did fun stuff with him, while I was stuck in the back seat watching. Ryan knew Buck had singled me out to intimidate, and he would pat me

---

Don't worry about the how—don't push your vision away.

---

on the shoulder and say, "You're going to get it," while I proudly fought back tears. That was bad, but it was the absolute worst being the only female in my class, coming closer to the end of that phase of training and still not being able to hover. I was last. LAST! I'd always come in first or second. I'd never felt as though I was a failure in my life.

Each night I went to my quarters, looked out the window and let the tears come. My heart wanted to give up, but my mind, my logic, my will would not let me quit, no matter how miserable I was. Then Buck went on vacation, and we got a new instructor for two weeks. He was patient, and showed me how to hold my elbows against my body so my hands wouldn't jerk the controls. One simple tip and I was up in the air at last! I could do it!

The greatest triumph of my life was being able to finish that phase—IN LAST PLACE—and stay with my class as we advanced to instrument training. There was no ceremony or anything like that; I shook my commander's hand before moving on to a different area of the flight line. But, that simple handshake was huge—this time I had accomplished something that was REALLY challenging. I fulfilled my vision—I became it. My favorite photo is of the first time I flew solo in flight school. Just you and your stick buddy do one flight around the traffic pattern, and it's like the Macy's Day parade.

Buck may have had a position of power as my instructor, but I did not have to allow him to control my destiny. I could have failed and blamed him and used that as an excuse, but I chose not to. Buck tried to limit me based on his belief that women didn't belong in his career. Let me tell you—limitations are only what someone else tries to impose on you. Never stop believing in yourself, no matter what anyone else says.

Don't worry about the how—don't push your vision away. After all, when God does things, He does them perfectly. So when God takes His energy and puts it into you as an idea or vision, isn't it perfect? Why question it? What is your life but a mystic quest? Why not enjoy the journey as you go? Just as I brought the *Army Officer Guide Book* to Basic, bring everything you need to see you through to the end. Assume you're moving forward and bring all your guides along.

I challenge you to be limitless; to *choose* to live your life to the fullest every day, without regret. When you do, you will soar further in your life.

Elizabeth McCormick has traveled the country as an inspirational speaker, relating the challenges faced in her years as a female BlackHawk Helicopter pilot and Chief Warrant Officer for the U.S. Army to everyday obstacles. She flew air assaults, rappelling operations, command & control missions and military intelligence-gathering flights. In 1999, Elizabeth supported United Nations peacekeeping operations in Kosovo. She was released from the military in 2001 after a career-ending injury.

Elizabeth is also a founding member of the John Maxwell Team and a certified coach, trainer and speaker, as well as an award-winning sales consultant. She has facilitated trainings at many national conventions and has been featured as a main stage speaker. Elizabeth also coaches entrepreneurs on how to improve their marketing reach, social media brand and sales strategies using systems and technology. Listen to her Soaring Further *radio show at www.SoaringFurther.com and connect with Elizabeth at www.YourInspirationalSpeaker.com.*

Take the Leap of Faith

Lisa Chell

Whenever my husband brings up the subject of moving, my response is always the same: "I'll live anywhere on the planet, as long as I can swim." When I need to find peace, I go to the water. It's part of who I am and how I exist. Swimming is a moving meditation as I breathe and move, breathe and move, breathe and move, challenging myself physically as I let everything else wash away.

My childhood summers were spent camping at a lake in Northern Saskatchewan. I would jump in the lake at seven a.m. and stay in all day, my parents dragging me out at dark. By the time I was a teenager I swam competitively, pushing past my limits for the pure joy of it. I put myself through college working as a lifeguard, and kept swimming and racing, no matter how my life and priorities changed.

Despite my love of the water, I still felt a bit like a loser when, at the age of thirty-seven, I found myself working part-time at a swimming pool, trying to figure out what to do with my life. I had left my career in medical laboratory technology to stay at home with our children. I loved my family dearly, but being a homemaker was not my calling. Even though I felt aimless , I loved the work at the pool and the people. Every day I dove into my peace-place and let it all go—breathe, move, breathe, move, breathe, move.

When our small, resource-based community was hit with a recession, I was the driving force behind a fundraising project for new equipment and programs that would keep the people in the pool and the doors open. The Fun, Fitness and Families initiative raised almost $250,000, and the pool was busy and lively. After the mayor and town councilors recognized me with an award, my lovely boss approached me and said, "The municipality supports and encourages succession planning for salaried staff. I'm leaving in six years, and I think you'd be a perfect fit to step into my shoes."

What? You mean I could have a career doing what I love the most? My heart was bursting. I thought, "Maybe this is the message I am getting from God: to take something I have always loved and

---

What? You mean I could have a career doing what I love the most? My heart was bursting.

---

really go for it. Maybe I could bring that love I've always felt for this environment and share it in a huge way with the community." Me? Aquatic Supervisor? *Yes.* It felt right.

I listened intently as my boss gave me a list of recommended courses and the certifications I would need for the job. She said, "We can't fund your training, so if you want this, you have to go for it on your own."

That was easy! I had found my passion and I would do anything to make it happen.

Over the next few years, I spent thousands of dollars on training; put in hundreds of hours of study, training and practicum work; and contributed hundreds of volunteer hours to continue fundraising for the pool. I wrote articles for the paper and gave interviews for radio and local TV. Just as when I swam in the lake all those years ago, I came in early and stayed late, loving every minute of it.

Six years later, I was ready. My goals were set, my training complete, and I felt confident in my abilities and my understanding of what made our team so great. Then it happened. Just a few weeks before she was to leave, my boss came to me in tears. "Management just announced—there will be no Aquatic Supervisor. They're eliminating my position." I felt as if somebody had reached into my chest, ripped out my heart and stomped on it, right in front of me. After six years of dreaming, working, studying and living my passion, the heartache was too much. It was huge for me, as if someone died.

To make matters worse, after all of the years of training and giving my heart to the pool, the pool had taken something from me—my feet. I had struggled for years with such acute inflammation and nerve issues in my feet that by the time the decision from management came down, I had already been walking with a cane, freezing my feet in ice just to get through a shift. I was literally left without a foot to stand on.

I was forty-four years old, off-deck, on disability, in physical therapy and living in a small town with limited opportunities to retrain in anything that even remotely interested me. I was completely heartbroken. For me, it was rock bottom.

I was literally left without a foot to stand on.

Every day I would lie in bed, blankets tucked under my chin, looking up through the skylight with tears in my eyes, asking God for a WOOWOO—Window of Opportunity, Wonder of Opportunities.

Intuitively, I knew God had not tricked me. "You didn't spend all of those years and all of that time, money and energy pursuing your passion just to have it mean nothing," I told myself. "Just be patient and wait for a sign."

One day after I shared my struggles with a friend, she said, "Why don't you use all of your knowledge in recreation as an instructor, trainer and coach in a different way?"

Her question reminded me that just because I had lost the position I had been working toward didn't mean that I had lost my passion, my knowledge or my experience. It was all still there.

41

For years, I had coached one of the biggest lifesaving clubs in Canada. When kids got discouraged because they lost a race, or believed they weren't "as good as" their friends, I would tell them my story of racing against my friend Dana. She was my best friend, and introduced me to competitive swimming when I was fourteen. We swam with a summer swim club and competed on the high school swim team together. In all of those years, I never once won a race against Dana. You want the people you love to be successful, but it was frustrating.

I would always end the story by telling the kids, "Even though Dana won every race, she eventually stopped racing. I never did. Winning or losing never stole my love of being in the water. If your happiness is based on whether or not you win a race, then you really don't love what you're doing. I still swim because nothing could ever kill that love. *Nothing*."

Recalling that story I had told so often, I realized that though I had lost my dream job, it was really just another race. Management couldn't take anything away from me at heart level—it wasn't for them to take, nor was it for me to give.

I've always believed that for every question in your life, *you* are the answer. So I tapped into my intuition and remembered

---

Maybe I could take all of my knowledge, gifts and expertise and apply them in a new way!

---

my secret dream to become a public speaker. The dream had always seemed too big, scary and impossible. How would I do it as the mother of four living in a small town? "Perhaps this is the WOOWOO I've been asking for," I thought. Maybe I could take all of my knowledge, gifts and expertise and apply them in a new way!

Even though the idea felt right and lit me up inside, I was scared to death. How was I going to go from bathing suit to business suit? I was terribly insecure and worried that the whole world would know I was a fake. I felt like a middle-aged baby—everything was so new! But once I committed to taking the leap, the right people and opportunities just showed up and I took action. I invested in myself. I networked. I studied. I built relationships. I soaked everything up like a sponge. It was as if I was back at the lake, jumping in first thing in the morning and staying out until dark.

Today, I assist organizations and managers with their staff using a coach approach, and it's as natural a fit as swimming. I understand now that sometimes it's easiest to see your path when everything else has been stripped away.

When you feel as though you've lost "everything," all you have left is the core of who you are and one very important question: *What do I love?*

J.K. Rowling, author of the *Harry Potter* series, said, "Rock bottom became a solid foundation on which I rebuilt my life." When you "lose," when you hit rock bottom—even if your rock bottom isn't a tragedy, an accident or a crisis of life or death, but something as simple as not getting a job, or not knowing what to do with your life—it is an opportunity to build a new, better life. You begin by trusting your intuition, and by getting back to the core of who you are and what you love. It's from that core place that you will find the courage to take a leap of faith.

Remember, for every question in your life, *you are the answer.* No matter what happens, hang on to your passion, that thing that brings you peace and joy, that one thing that makes you want to get up early and stay out 'til dark. Breathe, move, breathe, move, breathe, move. And no matter what—keep swimming.

Lisa Chell is a Professional Certified Power Coach® and Group Power Coach® with Mind Kinetics®, and an accredited coach with the International Institute of Coaching. She specializes in coaching leaders, managers and decision-makers to lead with both logic and heart. Her training and coaching focuses on immediately usable ideas and tools that bring out the genius in teams. Lisa is an active member of the Canadian Association of Professional Speakers and has presented for a variety of organizations and conferences across the country. She is the proud mom of two daughters, Erika and Helena, and two sons, Kai and Liam, and is happily married to her loving and brilliant husband Joel. Her passion is to empower people to be conscious creators of happiness in all areas of their lives by being the leaders of their own lives first. Connect with Lisa at www.UltimateClarity.com.

The Power in Doing Things Fast

Lorelei Kraft

I wake to the sounds of hissing and crackling. It's been an especially hot, steamy August night, but it shouldn't be *this* hot. I look out my bedroom window and see that the building next to my house, which contains my entire candle-making business, is utterly engulfed in flames.

It takes a frantic split second for me to remember that the kids are visiting my sister in Wisconsin. *Thank God!* I race to the phone to call the fire department. It's midnight. *How long will it take for them to get here ten miles out in the woods? Will they make it before the house catches on fire, too?*

I rush outside to hook up a hose. The candle building is a roaring inferno; clearly it is a lost cause already. So, I concentrate on hosing down the house, praying it won't catch fire. In between my frantic dousings, I race back inside the house to carry out the belongings that are most precious to me: photos of my children and paintings I have done over the years. When the pump in the well house blows from the heat and I lose all water power, I stand between the burning building and my house, sweat streaking the soot on my face, and scream at the sky, "Not my house too, God— NOT MY HOUSE TOO!"

I started making candles in my basement in Green Bay, Wisconsin when I was pregnant with my second child. It took six years to get out of the basement, but by that time my business was doing well enough that my family moved to eighty wooded acres in northern Minnesota to live our dream of rural independence. We moved all our belongings in an old trailer, which then doubled as our starter home, and built an oversized garage next door to it in which I made my candles. Shortly thereafter, my husband and I divorced. I was on my own in the middle of nowhere with a fledging business and two small children to support.

The fire swept through my life just a year and a half after the dissolution of my marriage. The business was a total loss, burned down to the ground. The fire was so intense and huge that the firefighters told me later they had seen the fireball from two miles

The next morning I stood alone and surveyed the smoking, smoldering ruins.

away. It was an absolute miracle that my home just fifteen feet away had survived with only a cracked window and a film of soot to scrub away.

The next morning I stood alone and surveyed the smoking, smoldering ruins. I didn't shed a tear but started organizing the cleanup. And I got on the phone to my suppliers: "Send me wax; send me molds; send me wicking!"

I was surprisingly calm—until the head of the savings and loan that held my mortgage called me to scream accusingly, "You better have insurance!"

I was so shocked by his insensitivity that I burst into tears. "I do," I choked, and hung up. That was the only time I cried over what had happened. Instead, I put all the energy that could have gone into weeping and wailing into building my business again.

I didn't cry over the devastation of the fire, but as I took twilight walks down the country roads, I did a lot of questioning. *Why did this happen to me? Why now, so soon after the divorce?* I had always felt safe in the world, and now this physical place had been ripped away from me too. Why hadn't the Universe protected me from this disaster? Even during that time of deep questioning in my soul, however, I was already beginning again. I didn't let the disaster paralyze me or prevent my feet from moving forward to rebuild my life.

And something wonderful came from the fire. I built a bigger building. Because I had a bigger building, I had room to create a small store in one corner.

The adventure of finding my candle "factory" in the middle of the northwoods created an attraction for tourists. Because the tourists spent so much money when they came, I began to visualize an entire "village" of handcrafts, featuring pottery, woodworking, candle-dipping, stained glass, jewelry and other items made by craftspeople I knew and admired.

Our poor, rural area suffered from a staggering twenty-percent unemployment rate. I found other women who could also see this dream of creating employment, a market for local crafts and even possibly a tourist attraction. We incorporated as "Founding Mothers, Inc.," just twelve ordinary women who worked as teachers, nurses, community volunteers—and one candlemaker!

However, none of us had any experience in building a project of this magnitude—and we had less than six weeks if we were going to be open by the beginning of tourist season, Memorial Day

> *I didn't let the disaster paralyze me*
> *or prevent my feet from moving*
> *forward to rebuild my life.*

weekend. The locals called us "crazy," and the "experts" told us we'd never be able to coordinate it all in six weeks. We had to get the infrastructure built on sixty-seven acres of wilderness—road, electricity, well and septic system; build eight "cottages;" hire and train sixty people to staff the buildings; find two hundred crafters to supply handwork to the shops; create an inventory system; display the crafts in the cottages; and quickly put together a tourist brochure on a place that didn't exist yet!

Fortunately, I've never let "reality" stand in my way. Just as with the rebuilding after the fire, I moved quickly with developing plans to build the village. Despite the naysayers, The Village of the Smoky Hills was built and opened in just *five weeks and five days* from the day we broke ground! An article in *Corporate Report Minnesota* said, "What the Founding Mothers did would blow the hardhat off of any general contractor." Our village became a major Minnesota tourist attraction. In its first year, it had one-hundred-

You're going to have to get up eventually anyhow—you might as well do it quickly!

thousand visitors and won all the top Minnesota tourism awards. It eventually employed one hundred people, and sold the handwork of four hundred artisans. The economic impact on the local area was astounding.

I truly believe that the Universe unfolds in its own time and in its own way. Sometimes doors have to close so that new ones can open. Sometimes the old has to be cleared away to make room for the new. The two worst things that happened to me—my divorce and the fire—had to happen to make me the person I am today and to open the door for the village to come into being. My life started getting better the day I stopped saying, "Why is this happening to me?" and started saying, "What am I supposed to be *learning* from this?"

The faster you get back on your feet when something bad happens, the better off you are. Start moving before it sinks in, and by the time it *does* sink in, you'll already have moved forward enough that you won't become paralyzed or find yourself curled up in a fetal position. You'll already be off and growing again.

I didn't allow myself time for a pity party when I saw there was virtually nothing left of my only way to support my children—I went into action by calling suppliers. By the time I was able to really grasp the extent of the devastation, I was already rebuilding. The grief over what I had lost was minimized by the progress I had made toward rebuilding the new. You're going to have to get up eventually anyhow—you might as well do it quickly!

Success, to me, is taking your vision and turning it into concrete reality—followed by meeting the challenge of making other people see and want what you envision. On every level, the joy is in creating! The true measure of success is not to be found in money, or glory or fame, but in happiness and satisfaction with what you do. I found great joy in meeting the challenge of rebuilding after the fire, and pulling all the threads together to make it all work again. Despite the devastation, I found joy in creating again from the ashes. And there was equal joy in starting with nothing but an idea and turning it into a "village!"

There will be things in life that you can't put back together. That's okay—turn and go in the direction of the things you *can* do. In spite of everything, you can get up and move forward quickly. And, when you create something new, as we did in building the village, again move quickly. Nothing is impossible. So, never let "reality" stand in your way—you alone determine what your reality will be. Life may not ever be perfect, but you can make it fuller, richer and happier, no matter what obstacles you meet, by the attitude you take.

As a single "mom-entrepreneur" who started from scratch with no training, Lorelei Kraft has created numerous odds-defying businesses, including two multi-million dollar ones. She built the award-winning craft village from scratch in an astounding five weeks and five days, and her businesses have brought $53 million in revenues, 610 employees and half a million visitors to her poor, rural county. A motivational speaker on leadership and innovation, she developed her "Seven Keys to Anything is Possible!"™ system to challenge others to see a world of unlimited possibility.

Lorelei is a Minnesota Woman Business Owner of the Year, recipient of the Governor's Entrepreneurship Award, winner of the National Organization of Women Business Owners Vision Award and president of the Million Dollar Mamas Club. She is the producer of Five Weeks and Five Days, *a documentary about building The Village of the Smoky Hills that was chosen as a PBS special. Lorelei is the top-selling author of* Letting Go of Mommy Guilt: Minnesota's Woman Business Owner of the Year Shares Her Secrets of How You Can Raise Good Kids Even If You're Super Busy! *as well as* Anything Is Possible! What You Can Learn From a Little Country Girl Who Went From a Two-Room School to Building an Award-Winning 'Village' From Scratch in Just Five Weeks and Five Days. *She is co-author with Brian Tracy and others of* Jump Start Your Success! 23 Top Speakers Share Their Insights for Creating More Success, Wealth and Happiness. *Connect with Lorelei at www.LoreleiKraft.com and www. MillionDollarMamas.com.*

Damaged Goods

Jeanie Douthitt

It's New Year's Eve, I'm driving in the biggest ice storm ever to hit Texas, and I've just left my husband. My friend Linda, who flew to Illinois to help me pack up my life, is asleep in the seat next to me; my seven-year-old son, Shane, is asleep in the back. I know I've made the right decision, but my heart is filled with sadness, and my mind races with worry.

I'm thinking about my husband Terry, knowing that leaving the abusive situation was the right decision, but missing him just the same. And I'm thinking about the fact that I am moving to Dallas—a city I've only visited once—with no job, no place to live, and four hundred dollars in my pocket. *How am I going to make it on my own? What if I have to go back?*

Suddenly, the trailer jackknifes, and I lose control of the car. Images from my past flash before my eyes, too fast to register. *Oh my God, we're going to die!* It all happens so fast. Within seconds, we are in the ditch by the side of the road. The trailer is banged up, but we are safe.

Later, as I watch the tow truck pull my car and the trailer out of the ditch, I wonder if this is a sign, further evidence that I am being punished. Words I've heard since I was a young woman flash through my mind and enter my weary, tender heart: "You are damaged goods. You made your bed; now you have to lay in it."

Again, my mind races with questions and fearful thoughts. *I haven't even made it to Dallas yet, and I've already had a wreck. Maybe I am "damaged goods." Maybe I'm not good enough. Maybe I am living the life I deserve. Maybe I can't make it without Terry. Maybe I should just turn around and go back.*

I think back to the first time someone called me "damaged goods." I was sixteen, an "unwed mother" in the mid-1960s, when teenage pregnancy was considered an unspeakable shame for a family. Unwed mothers were society's outcasts, and their babies

---

"You are damaged goods. You made your bed; now you have to lay in it."

---

were labeled "illegitimate." Despite the fact that I had never been intimate with anyone other than my boyfriend; despite the fact that we came from respectable, middle class families; despite the fact that I was a good girl on the honor roll, was vice president of my class and on the student council, I was labeled "promiscuous."

It took me six months to get up the nerve to tell my parents I was pregnant. I hadn't gained any weight, so I was able to hide the pregnancy. I was terrified to tell my father, the man who had doled out harsh punishments for my "bad" behavior.

I remember a time when my sister and I went to the neighbor's house to play, and forgot to tell my mom we were going. She was petrified, because she didn't know where we were. When she finally found us she said, "When your Daddy gets home, you are going to be in *big* trouble."

After he was told what we did, he gave us a choice: "You can have a spanking with the belt, or you can be grounded for a week."

My sister chose to be grounded, but I said I would take the spanking instead. After I got the belt he said, "You're grounded, too. That will teach you to take the easy way out."

When I finally told my parents I was pregnant, they made it very clear that they were mortified, disgusted and ashamed. They immediately called my boyfriend's parents, who assumed I must have talked him into having sex. Our parents decided it wasn't a good idea for us to get married, and then my boyfriend and his parents basically washed their hands of the situation. Suddenly, it was up to me to make the decision to keep the baby or consent to an adoption. I had never felt so alone or scared in my life.

My parents told me I would be punishing my baby if I kept him. "You won't be able to find a job to take care of him, or finish high school," they said. "You are 'damaged goods.' No man will ever want you."

My father told me to stay in my room when he was at home. "I don't want to look at you," he said. I became a prisoner in my own room, so depressed that I tried to make myself have a miscarriage by taking castor oil and falling down a flight of stairs.

The night my son was born, I was in hard labor for several hours, crying because the pain was unbearable. My mother said, "You should have thought about what you would have to go through before you went and got pregnant." *You made your bed; now you have to lay in it.*

When my son was born, I heard him cry, but I never got to see him, or hold him in my arms. I was told he was a healthy baby boy. I missed the feel of him inside me, and I hoped and prayed that he went to a loving home. Everyone around me convinced me that I had made the best decision for my baby and me. They said I would forget, but I never did. There hasn't been a day in forty-six years that I haven't thought about him.

A few months before my high school graduation, I ran into my boyfriend again while visiting my hometown with my sister and her husband. He and I went to dinner that night, and talked all night about what had happened. I couldn't believe how quickly those old feelings came back for us. He admitted that he hadn't wanted to give up the baby and that his parents had influenced his actions. Over the next several months, we talked on the phone and wrote letters to each other. It wasn't long before we decided to get married. Yes, my first boyfriend and my husband Terry are one and the same—the father of both my sons.

We married a few days after my graduation. Five years into a very happy marriage, we decided to start a family. It was a joyful time, but a difficult pregnancy. I remember praying, "I want this baby so badly. Please let it be a boy." There was such a big hole in my heart for the child I gave up, and I believed that, somehow, having another boy would help me heal that hole. When Shane was born, I was on top of the world. I never thought I could love anyone the way I loved him.

But our happy times didn't last. After we had been married for nine years, Terry started drinking a lot. He would hang out in bars, sometimes staying out until the wee hours of the morning. He was verbally abusive, and this evolved into physical abuse. I stayed, partly because I hoped things would get better and I wanted a

Now, after wrecking the car, I'm sure I have to turn back to the life I once created for myself.

stable home with two parents for Shane; but I also stayed because I really didn't think I deserved more, or better, or any different from exactly what I was getting. Every day I heard or felt my parents' admonishment: "You are damaged goods. You made your bed, now you have to lay in it."

One night Terry said, "The only reason I married you was because my parents thought it was the right thing to do." Just like the moment I had to give our first son away, my heart broke into a thousand tiny pieces. *Things will only get worse if you stay*, I thought. But how could I survive, raising Shane on my own? The decision was made when Terry came home drunk one night and knocked me across the room. I knew I had to take Shane and leave. I decided to move to Dallas, where my good friend Linda lived. I called her, and she flew up to Illinois that day and helped me pack up the U-Haul trailer.

Now, after wrecking the car, I'm sure I have to turn back to the life I once created for myself. *Is this the life I signed up for when I got pregnant? Is the wreck confirmation that I deserve to be punished?*

When I wake up in the hotel room the next morning to find the sun shining and the roads clear, I know I made the right decision in leaving. *I may be "damaged goods," but I have to keep going.* Within our first two weeks in Dallas, I find a job and an apartment—and just like that, Shane and I have started our new life.

Within a year, I am working for IBM, where I stay for twenty years. The feeling of not being worthy, or good enough, never leaves me. It's a hard label to shake. But there are moments of grace, moments when I have a glimpse of my true self: the good girl, the capable, powerful woman underneath all of my shame. The day I buy my first home is a huge milestone for me, because I never thought I could do it on my own. That's when I realize: *I don't have to settle for less than, or second best. I deserve this.*

It was that milestone of home ownership that inspired me to get into real estate several years later. When I started in real estate, I knew I wanted to focus on helping single women purchase their

---

No matter what we've done in the past, or how others label us, we are all entitled to a beautiful life.

---

own homes. I could relate to where many of them were coming from. Even if they didn't feel they were "damaged goods," many had their own labels or fears to overcome. I helped them work through their frustrations and push past their fears. Above all, *I treated them with respect and showed them they didn't have to settle.*

When the first woman told me, "You don't just help women buy homes; you change women's lives," I knew what my purpose was: to help women buy their own piece of "The American Dream." Purchasing a home on my own gave me a sense of empowerment I had never felt before, and I wanted other women to experience that feeling.

It took me a long time to realize that *I am not damaged goods* and to shift my perception of the choices I made in my life. Giving up my firstborn to a loving home, getting out of an abusive marriage—these are successes, not choices for which I should feel ashamed. We don't have to settle for "less than" as some sort of eternal punishment for past "misdeeds." No matter what we've done in the past, or how others label us, we are all entitled to a beautiful life.

Jeanie Douthitt is an award-winning, top-selling realtor and founder of "Smart Women Buy Homes," a program that assists single women who want to purchase homes solo. Partnering with both a mortgage and title company who share her values, Jeanie's program eases the intimidation factor when making the decision to own a home, guiding clients through the process from start to finish and empowering them to push past fear and self-doubt to independently purchase their own piece of "The American Dream."

After twenty years in the information technology industry and a successful career at IBM, Jeanie applied her sales and marketing experience, tenacity, focus and passion for making dreams come true quickly to a new career in real estate. In her first year as a realtor, Jeanie was named to the Coldwell Banker International Diamond Society, a membership limited to the top twenty-one percent of nearly one hundred thousand Coldwell Banker sales associates worldwide. She was also named to the President's Circle 2007-2011, the top four percent of all Coldwell Banker sales associates. In 2009, Jeanie was named the #1 Top Individual Sales Associate for Coldwell Banker Apex, Realtors. She co-authored the book Networking for Novices, and for the last two years was named one of the top real estate agents in Dallas-Fort Worth by dMagazine. Connect with Jeanie at www. SmartWomenBuyHomes.com.

The Beautiful Answer

Bobby J. Bryant

I stood there holding my 9mm pistol, crying so hard that I gagged as I pushed the gun further and further into my mouth.

Life had seemed so dark and empty for so long, I wanted more than anything to be able to pull that trigger and kill myself, like my best friend Danny had just days earlier. After losing both Debbie and Danny, I had nothing. Suicide seemed like my only option, a beautiful answer to an ugly question.

But, I couldn't do it. I just couldn't bring myself to pull the trigger. Utterly defeated and disgusted with myself, I uncocked the pistol and threw it on the bed. At that moment, I realized that I was more afraid of dying than I was of living my cold and hateful life.

Just a few months before, Debbie, who was wearing my ring, had moved out and left me for another man. We'd been together off and on (but mostly on) for twelve years, since I was a kid of eighteen and she was a worldly older woman of twenty-two. Our relationship was passionate and tumultuous. She was beautiful and confident and the whole world to me. We were apart for two years, in the middle of our relationship. During those two years, all my decisions were still based on her: thinking about her, wanting to please her, wanting to be with her and wanting to be like her. I used to joke that I spent one hundred percent of my time making

Debbie happy, and she spent one hundred percent of her time making herself happy—which left nobody there for me.

When Debbie left, everything left. Every happiness, every memory of my adult life left. I felt like a child, a babe in the woods. I was totally lost and, for three months, I couldn't even work. I spent all my savings on my bills and stayed in the house with the curtains closed. *Titanic* had just come out on cable, and I watched it two or three times a day and cried, cried so hard I thought I would die from the pain. Trying to find a port in the storm, I started reading everything I could get my hands on. I looked for stories that were as sad as my own—that would show me I was not alone—but I could find none. I couldn't believe what Debbie

---

I just couldn't bring myself to pull the trigger.

---

had done to me. It seemed that she was the root of all evil, but I couldn't fathom life without her. There was just nothing.

I couldn't bear to touch our bed, so I made one up in the living room and slept there for three months. I couldn't imagine talking to anyone or anyone talking to me. My mom often drove by to check and see if the lights were on, if I was still alive. During those three months, I left my house a total of five times. Each time, the person who managed to get me out was my best friend and only confidante, Debbie's brother Danny.

Danny was my solace, but he was facing a lot as well. We were both in construction and he had been accused of stealing from a job. He had contracted Hepatitis C from shooting heroin with a dirty needle. Although drugs were not my thing, I spent a lot of time with Danny. He sometimes shot up while we were driving. It was obvious that we were both in a very dark place. It didn't take long for our conversations to turn to how much we both wanted to die, for it all to be over.

One day, Danny called. "I just got back to my house," he said. "I was driving over to your place with two syringes full of crank, cocaine and heroin." Silent, I waited for him to finish. "I thought we could just go to sleep and never wake up." To this very moment, I do not know what I would have done if he had come over.

"Why did you go back home?" I asked. "Why didn't you come over?" He never answered my question.

Two days later, Debbie called. She was hysterical. "Danny shot himself. He's dead." I raced to the house where Danny and their father lived. The police were present, and Danny's room had been closed off and labeled a crime scene. I spent the next five days comforting Debbie, her dad and her new boyfriend. Those who cared about me the most tried to tell me it was unhealthy for me, but it was good to be with her and good to be needed, no matter the circumstances.

At Danny's wake, I heard people asking, "How could he do this to his family and those who care about him?" I, better than anyone, understood exactly how he felt—how, when the darkness has blinded you to the light, ending it all seems like the only answer. Later that day, I found myself in the backyard, screaming, "How could you leave me here?" I've never been so angry at anyone in my

---

Life was heavy, and I was just so tired.

---

life. He found the blueprints for suicide and didn't share them with me. He found a way to raise that gun to his head and actually pull the trigger, and he didn't tell me how.

Christmas passed. New Year's passed. Things got even worse. Danny was gone. Debbie was gone, and I was alone. I got the flu and stopped eating. I was a mess—I was hoping to die in my sleep, trying to die without having to do it myself, hoping something would just take me away. Life was heavy, and I was just so tired. That's when I found myself standing in the dark with a gun in my mouth, unable to pull the trigger.

I was losing my mind; I was falling apart. One night, out walking in my neighborhood, I started screaming in the middle of the street, calling God out. "You're useless!" I yelled. "If You're really there, it's time to show up!" Imagine that, God didn't appear.

So I put out the ultimatum, "God, Devil, whoever shows up first, I'm in. God, You show up first and I'll be Your right-hand man, I'll help You save the planet and be the light of the world. Devil, if you show up first I will stand with you. I will help you destroy everything and bring darkness into the world." I was angry and I wanted answers, but no deity from either side appeared before my eyes that night.

One day, just after putting my gun in my mouth for the second time and being once again unable to pull the trigger, I remembered an experience I'd had three years before, just before Debbie moved out and before I knew about her new man. She, my mom and I were out to dinner, and I went outside on the patio with my coffee

---

I realized I had had a choice all along.

---

to let them talk privately for a moment. The Dave Mathews Band was playing on the radio, the sun was setting and a cool breeze was blowing. It was perfect.

Suddenly, I had an amazing epiphany: Every happiness I had ever experienced was based on something outside of myself. At that moment, I knew deep in my soul that life was going to be okay. *Everything will be okay—not because she will stay or leave; not because of a new job, a new car or money in the bank, but because I can choose. Everything is going to be okay—everything is okay right now.* It was a beautiful thing. God was right there. I knew right then, proof positive, that the answer had finally arrived. It wasn't until three years later—when that beautiful experience had long been only a memory—that I realized my grand epiphany had been a ray of sunshine through the clouds, a new understanding and a turning point I had ignored. This time, I took the lesson. I began to pursue a different path.

Once I started to figure out some sort of purpose for my life, I realized I had had a choice all along. I was creating my darkness because I didn't have a sense of self. I was living for something outside myself, and once that something was gone, I was gone. I now understand, firsthand, that people who want to kill themselves do it. People who *talk* about it are trying to find a different way to live.

Where I live my life now, that gun is a gift. I'll never forget how close I came to ending my life. If I had, I would never have become the man I am today. I'm a force to be reckoned with, and I'm a gift to those around me because the many challenges in my life have helped me find understanding and compassion for those in need of a new direction and a helping hand. I am a gift because I have the guts to share what I have been through. I still have dark days, and once in a great while I still have fleeting thoughts about death. I choose to stay here. I do not have to succumb.

The minute we understand the truth about choice, it becomes very clear that every thought, every word and every action is a choice. There are no have-tos in life. We *get to*, we *want to*—but we don't *have to*. Everything, in life, is a choice. That is the beautiful answer we are all searching for.

Bobby J. Bryant is an author, speaker and multi-talented entrepreneur. He is also living proof of what can happen when one decides to walk the path toward happiness. He lives a fulfilling life in Reno, Nevada where he is active in many different charities and nonprofits and gives frequent talks. Bobby is the author of the book Your Life, Your Choice: A Journey Toward Inner Peace *and the creator of* Extra, *a five-part CD audio series with matter-of-fact messages about taking responsibility for life choices. Connect with him at www.RadicalBobbyJack.com.*

I Get To Be Here

Deanna L. Robinson

My head feels as though it has literally exploded. Could this be an aneurysm?

My husband, Dave, assures me I wouldn't be this coherent and rushes me to the emergency room. The examining physician orders an MRI after looking at my CAT scan. Nothing seems to show up, so they send me home with pain medication.

But, the excruciating pain continues. *There's nothing wrong with me*, I tell myself. *I just have a really, really bad headache.* All I want to do is lie down, but I have a six-month-old; my youngest son is turning three; and I have three school-age kids, too. With this intense pain and no explanation, I just try to go about my daily activities with Dave's help and give thanks for the small blessings. *Thank God I'm not nursing anymore. I wouldn't want Emma to get all this medication I'm taking.*

The pain is all-encompassing. Any sound hurts. My neck is so tense my shoulders draw up to my ears. *If this isn't anything serious, what IS it?* I decide I'd better get a second opinion from a neurologist; I have no choice but to book an appointment six weeks out. So, for six more weeks I try to attend to a normal life while I walk around feeling as if a bomb has gone off inside my head.

At my appointment with the neurologist, I ask, "What was it they saw on the CAT scan that made them order the MRI? There's really *no* explanation for why my head is still hurting like this, for why I feel so awful?"

He throws the CAT scan up. "Hmmm," he says. "Well, I don't have your MRI right here. Why don't you go home, and I'll call you when I've had a chance to give it a look?" It is only twelve minutes from the hospital to my house. When I get home, the neurologist has already reached my husband to say, "You need to get back here. We need to do an emergency EEG." *WHAT?*

We race back and he tells us, "There actually is something. It looks like a hemorrhage. In fact, it's amazing you're still alive."

It is too frightening, too much to take in all at once. *Okay, so there* is *something. I suffered a cerebral hemorrhage. Usually, this kills people. I might still die if they open me up. I might still die if they don't. There are risks with an EEG. I might have another*

"In fact, it's amazing you're still alive."

---

clot. I might hemorrhage again. I'm reeling from all the medical terminology. Statistically, I shouldn't even be here. *How could they have missed THIS? How could I be walking around? What if I never see my kids again?*

The doctors want to start prepping me for blood work and an EEG right away. I can sense everyone's anxiety; there is real fear in their eyes. They have really messed up, and now they want to do damage control. But, I am not ready. "No," I say, "I don't think you understand. I've walked around like this for SIX WEEKS. It was not my time. Now you find a room where my husband and I can go make some phone calls."

I'm given a room where I pray, "God, I know You have a plan for my life. Pour out Your Holy Spirit upon us, the doctors and all those responsible for my care. Please give peace to Dave. Take care of my children. God, PLEASE!" I call my father-in-law to come and be with Dave. I don't want him to have to wait alone.

I call the couple staying with my kids, very good friends and fellow Christians, and tell them, "I need to pray with you." We pray together, and I tell them, "I need you to call everyone you can think of and put me on every prayer line."

Then I make calls to my pastor and my husband's priest. Connected in prayer, I feel a great sense of calm. "Okay," I tell the hospital staff. "I'm ready. Let's go."

In an EEG, they go in at your femoral artery, right at your hip, and move along through your carotid artery into your neck, scanning, shooting pictures and looking at the images, which are dyed to indicate where blood is flowing. I'm lying flat on the table in my hospital gown, and about a half hour in, tears start rolling out of my eyes and onto the table. A doctor asks, "Are you feeling some discomfort? Are you feeling pain?"

"No," I say. "I have five children. And I just wonder—are they ever going to see their mom again? Do I get to raise my kids?" *Will they get to know all I want to teach them? Will they ever know how much I love them, that I would do any and everything for their benefit?*

I told our eight-year-old daughter, Haley Sue, "I'm just going for some tests—I'll see you in the morning." *If she doesn't see me in the morning, what will it do to her in the long term? What if, every time someone goes to the doctor, it'll be just like her mom is never coming back?*

They have these enormous C-clamps, like people use in wood shops, to clamp me to the table. "You cannot move for eight hours, or you could bleed out or have a stroke," I am told. Then I am taken up to the ICU. Dave needs to get home and be with the kids, and none of my kids can see me in the ICU because they're too young. So I make a couple of phone calls from the table to tell them, "Mommy had some tests. I need to stay the night and sleep here. I'll talk with you tomorrow."

In the morning, I call Haley Sue to say, "I'm sorry I'm not home yet. When your class says morning prayers, just pray for Mommy."

In a small voice, she says, "Are you going to be okay?"

I can't bring myself to lie to her. We *don't* know if I am going to be okay. So I say, "You know what, honey? I think I am. I think this is going to be okay. What really matters is that God has a plan for us. Whatever happens, we are blessed. And that means that whatever happens, you don't need to be afraid." As I speak the words, I feel how deeply I truly believe them.

Overcoming adversity isn't about surviving the hemorrhage. It's the attitude that I've adopted with the years of struggle since then and how I view the challenges, obstacles and adversity that continue in life.

Every moment after that hemorrhage was and has been an absolute gift and blessing. Twenty-eight doctors, twenty MRIs and thirty-two drugs later, there is an explanation for the hemorrhage: Fifth disease, brought on by the human parvovirus. Just after the

---

Overcoming adversity isn't about surviving the hemorrhage.

---

birth of my fifth child, my youngest son Luc and eldest daughter Haley Sue brought home the virus. I had worried about the health of my new baby and hoped that breastfeeding would protect her; for most kids, the virus passes quickly and without complication.

Little did I know, it would lead to weakened immune systems and serious future health complications for me; for my eldest daughter, who was later diagnosed with Lyme disease; and for my youngest son, who was diagnosed with Crohn's disease in 2011. Fifth disease didn't cause my children's conditions, but it created the right environment for their health to be compromised.

There is no explanation, though, for why I'm still here—other than, it wasn't my time. Over the past thirteen years, I've suffered recurring challenges with my health. The virus manifests in a number of ways, always including exhaustion and pain. I used to think that, if I could just get past the current medical challenge, I could get on with my life. I kept waiting. *When I feel better. When it's totally gone. When I'm a hundred percent.* Well, I don't know what one hundred percent is anymore! This may be exactly what health looks like, for me. Thank God I get to!

What has really made the difference is my consistent *choice* to view all that I experience as a blessing. I do not succeed every day, let me tell you, but I do try to focus on this: Whatever I experience, *I get to* experience. Negativity takes up way too much energy. For me, success is being able to live moment by moment in gratitude and joy. I believe someone can truly say, "I'm successful" when they make that turn to the positive. It does not matter what life throws at you—it's how you view it.

For example, my eldest son Terry has cerebral palsy. I can go from, "Oh my gosh, I have a handicapped child!" to, "What a blessing that I get to have this simple view of life!"

When someone said, "Oh, that has to be awful," I thought, *Really? It's not! Do you know what a blessing it is? All he does is love. He enjoys life.* It made me realize, as a young mother, that our

> *We aren't promised tomorrow; today is what we celebrate. Today is a gift. TODAY.*

children are not little charms on our bracelets. God gave us these kids—what a blessing! They make us who we are, and how lucky we are to have them.

When Luc was diagnosed with Crohn's, I thought, *Really?* But then: *Why* not *us?* Did we think we were through with challenges and obstacles? Luckily, because of my extensive experience with illness and alternative modalities, we were able to get Luc effective treatment right away. *Everything* is a gift. It's a little shift in view, from "Woe is me" to "Let's see how this can have a positive impact on our lives!"

There are huge blessings in the challenges and adversity. They are important. They are, in some way, a gift to you. We aren't promised tomorrow; today is what we celebrate. Today is a gift. TODAY.

If you want to try for "I get to" rather than the old "I have to," don't allow the negative in. If that means not reading newspapers or not watching the news, it's okay.

Try reading a positive, motivational, inspiring book for fifteen minutes every day. I start my day, every day, in God's word. Whatever your point of spiritual reference, find it and start your day with it. If you don't have spiritual beliefs, just find a great motivational book, something that resonates deeply with you.

Living in Colorado, we're in the beautiful Rocky Mountains. There's a ski resort a couple of hours away, and we usually ski it as a family. Recently, I got off the chairlift at the top of a little trail, with my ski helmet on what we call my "million-dollar head," and stood looking out to the west at the Continental Divide, the beautiful blue sky and all those snow-covered peaks. *Thank You, God, thank You. I get to see this beauty. I get to have a day of peace with my family, all having a fun time. Thank You—I get to be here.*

Deanna L. Robinson is committed to helping people overcome adversity through her work as an enthusiastic leader and motivational speaker. A mother of five, former community theatre actress and current entrepreneur, she now handles public relations for her husband's two growing dental offices and shares her hard-won wisdom through storytelling that motivates and reflects a blessed life. Connect with Deanna at www. DeannaLRobinson.com.

Life: From Meaningful to Significant

Ali Swofford, PhD

As my repossessed company car rolled down the driveway, I realized it was over. I was out of time, out of money, out of options and out of business. The dream of female athletes worldwide competing in Ladies First custom uniforms was now just a dead corpse in the trunk of the collection agency's car. I was bitterly disappointed—I thought having the right idea at the right time and giving a hundred and ten percent to make it happen was the key to success.

Now, after seven years of meeting challenges and overcoming obstacles only to end up broke, two-thousand miles from my nearest relative and with no clue as to what my life's purpose was meant to be, my perception had changed. Had I achieved the height of my potential at age twenty-seven?

Beginnings always shape your sense of confidence, and my childhood was the best. My parents provided unconditional love, strong values, encouragement and limitless opportunities for growth. They were both college graduates and teachers, so there was never a doubt that I too would pursue advanced degrees. Praise and recognition, in the form of academic and sports honors, came easily. A full ride to USC for grad school, coaching Olympic athletes at twenty-one, PhD at twenty-three, first women's athletic director at the University of Nebraska at twenty-seven—the ride up was exhilarating. Local media dubbed me "the golden girl," and I believed I could do anything I set my mind to and was willing to work hard enough for.

When I became women's athletic director at the University of Nebraska, it was the late seventies and Title IX, the law that people could not be excluded from any federally funded education program (including sports) based on gender, was really taking hold. Women's sports finally had some money, but what else did

I'd show them—I'd start my own company!

we have? Sized-down men's uniforms with no attempt at style, the armpits hanging down past bra lines, and skintight, straight-cut shorts. I was athletic director at an NCAA school—why couldn't I find a single comfortable, functional uniform designed for a woman's body to buy for my teams?

I talked to the women's athletic director at the University of Tennessee. "We have several textile manufacturers in Knoxville, and I know some of the people in the industry," she said. "Why don't you fly down here and talk to some of these big companies?"

I did, and was amazed to get the cold shoulder from the manufacturers. "We don't think this Title IX thing is going to be a big deal," they said, "and we really don't think there's a need for a division of our company to be devoted to women's uniforms."

I was stunned. Women's athletics not a "big deal?" I'd show them—I'd start my own company!

I found two gentlemen in the industry in Knoxville who thought I had a great idea. One told me he'd write a business plan and secure our financing; the other ran purchasing at the huge Standard Knitting Mills and knew the business inside and out. Thrilled that I was bringing another dream to fruition, I signed a contract to be vice president of sales and marketing of this newly formed company we called "Ladies First."

With an entrepreneur's fire in my belly, I quit my directorship at the University and moved to Knoxville, only to find that the first gentleman had dropped out without securing our financing. The other, Harold Finley, said, "Well, Ali, I'm real sorry about that contract. I'm going to have to keep my job at Standard Knitting Mills, at least for a while, till you and I see if we can get some financing and get Ladies First off the ground."

At twenty-nine, I thought I could do anything. Harold Finley and I put a good business plan together, found bankers that were willing to say, "great idea," and got Ladies First off and running. Of course, we were still just little fish in a big men's athletic pond, but I'd seen how one Oregonian's dream of an athletic shoe company had become a multi-billion-dollar phenomenon. I thought Ladies First would be the next Nike.

I spent the next seven years on the road. While our competitors flew their sales and marketing VPs to trade shows and put them up in fancy hotels, I drove from Knoxville to California, Illinois, Texas and all over the country. Wherever the shows were, there I was in my car with our samples in the trunk.

God wasn't mad; He just had another mission for my life that I had no idea he had been preparing me for.

We struggled through those years, always trusting we could make it work. Meanwhile, money in the business got tighter and tighter; bankers' shenanigans crashed the local economy; and credit for small business in Knoxville dried up. I was making less money than I had in high school. I started eating dinner at Happy Hour buffets and wondering where I'd find rent money. Finally, we had no further credit or savings left to give Ladies First a boost. The company car was repossessed, and we were forced to close the business and admit defeat. I was disappointed, confused and unfamiliar with failure, so I spent a lot of time asking, *Why did this happen? We did everything right! Is God mad at me? And, if this wasn't my purpose, what is?* God wasn't mad; He just had another mission for my life that I had no idea he had been preparing me for.

71

True, this golden girl was unaccustomed to failure; but, I'd seen my parents' example and knew challenges could be met head-on. Dad had deliberately repeated his senior year in high school four times because he couldn't afford college yet, but wanted to keep learning. Mom had multiple sclerosis all her adult life and taught on crutches or from a wheelchair. Both my parents were so strong. Did I have that same willpower?

I thought back to when the call came that my mom had died. I was twenty-three, just finishing my PhD and about to start a new job. In the course of a week, I lost my mom, planned a funeral, wrapped up my final dissertation, packed my bags and went from California to Texas to start a new life. I had risen to meet those challenges—why would I let Ladies First define me as a failure?

For a few years, I had been on the board of the Knoxville Women's Center, a volunteer organization that helped women re-enter the workforce. Our executive director and my dear friend, Annie Selwyn, had been diagnosed with terminal cancer. During her last months, I was amazed to witness the transforming effect her work with her financial planner, Wes Channell, had on her peace of mind. Her young son would be able to get the education she had planned for him after all. The plan could never replace his mother, but financial obstacles had been removed from his young life, and that made a huge difference to everyone.

An "ah-ha" moment! I realized I wanted to make that kind of difference in people's lives too. I decided to join Wes's financial firm. I discovered that it didn't matter that I was the only woman in my office, an unknown in the investment community and lacking formal training in finance; my talents, skills, values and learning experiences were transferable to this whole new sphere. I could communicate with people on their level and relate to their fears and dreams.

What I had learned from business, academics, sports and volunteering had prepared me to really help them. I was opening lines of communication between spouses and teaching financial and life discipline; I was creating paths through the jungle of risk, fear and uncertainty. Leading my clients to understanding, confidence and security as a partner felt fantastic. My life had gone from what I felt was a meaningful vocation to a life of significance. It's amazing what others can accomplish when you're passionate about helping them.

My mom's MS illustrates why my clients need disability protection. My dad's determination to get an education motivates me to help parents save for their children's education. Annie's story helps me show how life insurance changes lives. My seven years of being unable to save or put anything away for retirement resonates with small-business owners. Teaching skills help me explain how different investments work together to reach long-term financial goals. My passion for helping people see and solve their financial problems has a ripple effect that touches generations.

Life, like the financial world, is volatile; and it is tempting to focus on the short term, especially when things are bad. But, it's

---

My passion for helping people see and solve their financial problems has a ripple effect that touches generations.

---

not the sprint that matters. Even if you're at a tough point and aren't sure how you're going to make it, even if you're eating at the Happy Hour buffet, be open for the next opportunity.

Get involved in your community, place yourself around uplifting people and don't be afraid to say, "I'm struggling. I know I'm on a journey, but the path isn't clear. What do you see as my strengths? Where do you think those strengths could be applied in a meaningful way?"

Focus on your passions. When your life's work is not a job but a calling you'd do for free, you've discovered where your opportunity for significance lies.

Don't pigeonhole your talents, your skills or your experiences. Sometimes the "wall" we hit is merely God's way of showing us that what we have achieved in the past may have been meaningful, but what we will do in the future will go beyond meaningful to significant.

Ali Swofford, CLU, ChFC, and President of Swofford Financial since 1984, earned her PhD from the University of Southern California by the age of twenty-three. With previous experience as a college professor and coach in Texas and Women's Athletic Director at the University of Nebraska, Ali came to Knoxville in 1977 to start her own business. Since transitioning into personal wealth advising she has been the featured speaker on television, at national seminars and aboard international cruises. She has authored numerous financial articles. Her "Top of the Table" status places her among the world's top one percent of financial advisors. Having served on numerous nonprofit boards and given untold hours to the community, Ali was honored for her volunteer service when Knoxville named June 14 "Ali Swofford Day." Connect with Ali at www.SwoffordFinancial.com.

Into the Light

Connie Hertz

I couldn't believe my eyes. As I watched the second plane hit the World Trade Center in New York City from my living room in St. Paul, Minnesota, I was terrified. Like so many Americans who never imagined this destruction on our own shores, I felt my sense of safety slip away as smoke billowed from the top of Building Two.

But for me, the tremendously uneasy feeling that life would never be the same was compounded by the sudden destruction in my own life, as I watched Peter (I'll use that alias to protect his privacy), my husband of twenty years, pull into our driveway with a U-Haul truck. Just six days before, I discovered he had been having an affair. Just like that, my entire world fell apart.

It was too much, the national tragedy paired with my own crisis. I followed Peter from room to room, telling myself that I just wanted to make sure he didn't take anything of mine, when I really just felt so scared and lost. Our large, rambling house didn't feel like home; I didn't feel like *me*. *I don't know what to do. Who am I without the safety of this relationship, without my husband?* I felt as though someone had cut off my legs.

As I watched him load the last box and pull down the back door of the truck, with the sound of terror and confusion blaring from my TV set, I knew my marriage was truly over and life would never be the same.

I had felt this intense fear before, the night I discovered Peter had been secretly using IV drugs. Now, sitting on my couch alone, feeling as though I might actually have a nervous breakdown, I remembered that it had been almost exactly ten years since I woke up in the middle of the night to an empty bed, only to find Peter in the living room with drugs and needles splayed out on the coffee table.

That summer, Peter had barely come to bed at night. He was reserved, detached from the family, but it never occurred to me that he had started using drugs again. He had told me he was an IV drug addict in recovery when we met ten years before, the summer of 1981, but he seemed confident and strong, and his confession

*I knew my marriage was truly over
and life would never be the same.*

did not concern me. I was in love. He called me his "dream girl," and in turn I called him my "dream man." Most days, we proved each other right.

I really had no idea what addiction was, so I had no way of knowing that it was a disease, and that Peter could relapse at any time. So when I found him that night, desperate, sad and filled with guilt, it felt as though I had been hit repeatedly, all over my body, with a two-by-four. "I'll stop. I want to change," he said. I loved him so much, and I desperately wanted to make our marriage work, to help him, to keep our family together. So I agreed to stay and support him as best I could.

I wanted to believe Peter would get clean, that he *could* get clean, but I lived with an enormous, all-encompassing fear that he would not. I could barely think about anything else. *Is he using? Will he relapse again? Where is he? Is he buying drugs? What if he never gets better?*

I was so very ashamed. I didn't want our two children, aged nine and seven—or anyone else—to know what was happening in our home. I remember shaking with fear and anxiety, feeling colder than I've ever felt. I barely ate. I stopped taking care of myself, but did my best to hold myself together for the kids.

I lost weight, my gut tied up in knots, as our very dark secret grew into a very large monster. When I went to see a massage therapist to help me deal with the stress, she said, "You're so thin. What's going on?" I broke down, sobbing, and finally revealed the secret that had been tearing me apart. It was a small moment of relief, but enough of a taste of freedom from the darkness that I felt ready to face the harsh realities of Peter's addiction.

My husband went into a thirty-day treatment facility near our home in Indiana, and relapsed while in treatment. He was in the "chronic stages of his disease." We decided it would be best for him to attend treatment in Minnesota, at "the mothership of all treatment centers." After he completed his eight-month stay at the facilities there, we packed up and moved to St. Paul so he could be near the support system of his sponsor and other addicts in recovery. It was there that I found the help, the hope and the support I greatly needed in Al-Anon, a 12-step program for the loved ones of alcoholics and addicts, and faced my own issues around his addiction. It was also through Al-Anon that I discovered the leader within me, stepping up as the institution's Chair for two years and then as the Chairperson of St. Paul Al-Anon for three years. Through these leadership roles, I began to see myself outside of the role of wife and mother.

Dealing with drugs and addictive behavior is frightening; you don't know if your addict is ever going to come back. At the time Peter went into treatment, he was putting twenty-seven holes into his body every day. It was a miracle that he was able to pull himself out of the dark tunnel of addiction, get clean and *stay clean*, but he did. It was quite a feat, and amazing to watch. I was so proud of him for sticking with his own program and staying the course with his own recovery path.

But the addict's path is bumpy and sometimes treacherous, and those who love them know that, even when they're clean, they often exhibit the same behaviors they had when they were using drugs. Peter was angry for a lot of years, and there was a growing distance between us. We pretended it wasn't there. I pulled back emotionally and focused on my own Al-Anon program, and gave us the space I thought we both needed to heal.

Now, ten years after the night I found him high, surrounded by needles and drugs, I was right back in that darkness. Only this time, it seemed too much to get through. The pain of losing Peter and my family as I knew it—the pain of his betrayal—was so intense, I didn't care if I lived or died. Many times I said, "God, please send someone to kill me, because I can't do it myself. The

> *Now, ten years after the night I found him high, surrounded by needles and drugs, I was right back in that darkness. Only this time, it seemed too much to get through.*

pain is too much to take." Yet every time I said this, within half an hour someone would call me, or show up at my door to help me. Friends just kept showing up out of the blue exactly when I needed them, which helped to strengthen my faith in God. Somehow, with the support of friends and family and my Al-Anon meetings, I was able to at least keep on living. I didn't see the light at the end of this dark tunnel, but I hoped it would appear one day, just as it had before.

Almost two years after Peter left me, while participating in the Landmark Forum, a personal growth class, I listened to a man talk about how angry he was at his wife for having an affair. When he mentioned that it had been twenty-two years since it happened, my mouth dropped. Here he was, more than two decades later, estranged from his daughters and still so very bitter and angry, as if the affair had just happened. I started sobbing. *I'm still bitter, hurt and angry, too. If I don't change, I will end up just like this guy, and I will not let that happen.*

That day, the facilitator had me call Peter *in the class*. It was one of the hardest things I've ever had to do. I told him that I wanted to take full responsibility for my part in the downfall of our relationship. "It was self-preservation. I put up a protective wall, and I'm sorry I wasn't fully present when we were married," I said. The experience was scary, but also freeing. It was in that moment that I finally saw the light at the end of the dark tunnel, and that light looked a lot like freedom—freedom from pain and resentment toward him, but also freedom to step into my own power and become the woman I was always meant to be.

Once I saw the light, I just kept walking toward it. It wasn't always easy, but with the help of my support system, meditation and the new insights I was learning every day from great teachers and experts, I was able to come out the other side into a life that was beyond my imagining.

I remember standing in my beautiful new home—for which I designed and chose every single piece, right down to the cupboard knobs—and feeling tremendous joy. These feelings replaced any negative feelings I'd experienced up until that point, even the

> *No longer would I have to search for a tiny sliver of light at the end of a long dark, tunnel; in this house, in* my home, *the light would surround me.*

tremendous fear that gripped me on 9/11, when my world came crashing down around me. I said out loud, "This is me. This place is all me. I love my life! Thank you, God!" In stepping into my power, I had created a place where the sun would shine in every day. No longer would I have to search for a tiny sliver of light at the end of a long dark, tunnel; in this house, in *my home*, the light would surround me.

Hillary Clinton said it takes a village to raise a child, and I say we all need a village. We all need a team of people to help us to cope, to grow, to summon up the courage not only hold on until we see the light at the end of the tunnel, but also to go *toward* that light. Surround yourself with beautiful people who are positive, who give you energy, who bring out the best parts of you. Carefully select your team of people who will support you, love you, and give you strength, every step of the way.

Today, I am both a student and a teacher. I work weekly with my life/business coach, and I work weekly with my many coaching clients. I have lots of love and wisdom to give and to accept. I have stepped into my power, loving myself and knowing that I am a leader ready to inspire others to do the same. I have been in a loving, committed partnership with a kind man for eight years now, and I'm proud to say that Peter has been in recovery for more than twenty years.

Know that you too can walk through your dark tunnel. There will be light, if you just hang in there. Nothing is so horrible that you can't live through it. And when you reach the light, you will find you are stronger, more complete and more whole than ever before. Just keep walking. You'll get there; you will walk into the light.

Connie Hertz is a dream coach/life coach, founder of Essentially Youthful, LLC and a representative for Nu Skin Enterprises. A former oncology nurse, she applies her experience in wellness, health, nutrition, fitness and anti-aging to help people stand in their power and, no matter how old they are, become the best person they can be and live the most joyous life imaginable. Connect with Connie at www.ConnieHertz.com and www.ConnieHertz.NSEDreams.com.

Out of Great Loss Comes Great Faith

Mary Kay Sheets

Have you ever met someone you knew was going to have a lasting impact on your entire life as soon as you met her? Looking back, I only wish I could have known the extent of the impact one individual would have on my life.

I met Jana Backman in the summer of 1985, when she agreed to let Margo—a recent university graduate from England—live with her family for the summer. Margo and I were twenty and nineteen, respectively, when we first met; and we became fast friends while working together at the local KFC. Jana was thirty-seven. You couldn't find a more fun-loving, generous and friend-connected family than hers to hang with for the summer.

Jana, her husband Bill and son Eric all welcomed Margo and me into their family that summer as if we had always belonged. However, it was we girls who formed an incredible bond in those few months—sharing dinners; watching Jana's favorite "stupid" soap opera, *One Life to Live,* each night after work; and taking short trips together on the weekends.

To say it was hard to see the summer end and have Margo return to England is an understatement. It's never easy to say goodbye to a dear friend, even when you know you are destined to stay in each other's lives. We all have a friend like that in our lives—or, if we're lucky, even a few along the way.

Indeed, we all stayed in touch in the years to follow. I visited Margo in England that next summer. And Jana actually got me hired at the bookstore where she worked, while I also attended night school and worked a second job. We all remained incredibly connected and close.

It was about three years after Margo left that our lives changed dramatically. Jana was forty-two when she first faced cancer. Unfortunately, out of fear, Jana waited several months before mentioning the lump she had found. By the time it was diagnosed, she was in the advanced stages of breast cancer and had to have an immediate mastectomy. True to the amazing person she was, Jana was determined not to let the cancer win. She showed us all what it

---

We all have a friend like that in our lives—or,
if we're lucky, even a few along the way.

---

meant to be a warrior and not give up. Within several months, she had beaten the odds and had come through even more determined to live life to the fullest.

Our lives continued as they had that first summer until I decided that working two jobs and attending night school wasn't cutting it. I decided to attend the University of Nebraska-Lincoln to finish my degree. Once I left for college, Jana called me every Thursday. That was our day. I always knew it was her, even before I picked up the phone. "Is that you?" she'd ask.

"It's me! Is that you?" I would answer.

Jana could always make me laugh and feel her love of life. Whenever I found myself overwhelmed with work, school or life, it was my own mother and Jana who always called to lend their support or say, "You need to come home for a visit." They kept me moving forward.

Jana had lived five years cancer-free when it reared its ugly head for the second time; and it did so with a vengeance. Jana spent the next year engaged in a battle for her life, a battle she never let herself believe she could not or would not win.

In the spring of 1994, I was a month from graduating with a degree that Jana had always encouraged me to finish when I got *the call* from a dear mutual friend: "Mary, you need to come home," she said.

My heart dropped, and time stopped. I don't even remember leaving work, packing or getting in my car to head home. I only know that I drove the 370 miles from Lincoln, Nebraska to Moline, Illinois in less than five hours and that every second felt like an eternity.

The hallway outside Jana's hospital room was lined with family and dear friends. When I entered her room, Jana was bent over her bed table with her head resting on her arms, while Bill and a few close friends stood nearby ready to help in any way they could. Jana lifted her head to look up at me. She was clearly happy to see me, but confused as to why I was there and not at school. I sat down next to her and placed my arm around her back as she leaned forward to relieve her pain. I felt unimaginably helpless. I quickly realized: She doesn't know. She doesn't know she's dying.

I quickly realized: She doesn't know.
She doesn't know she's dying.

By late evening, Jana's condition had deteriorated greatly. She could not find physical comfort in any position and had grown agitated. "I want to go home now. Why can't I go home?" she kept asking. It was heart-wrenching. Jana grew so restless that Bill put her in a wheelchair and took her for a stroll through the halls to calm her. He wheeled her into the waiting room where I was sitting with their son, Eric. I looked up at Jana.

She looked at me, then up at the clock on the wall and then back into my eyes. She spoke a single word: "Shit."

In that moment, I saw her realize and understand that she would not be going home—at least not to any home she knew. I'll never forget her face at that moment. There was such deep sadness and a clear anger. I could almost hear her unspoken litany of regrets.

There were so many things she would never get to do now. She would never take that trip to visit Margo in England, see her son grow into a man or grow old with Bill.

"NO! I'm not ready," her eyes said to me. It was terrible to see her in such pain—it was the most devastating moment of my life. This willful woman, once so full of life, was simply not ready to let go of it. She wasn't ready to die. She had never even considered the possibility. She and Bill had never even had the conversation. They had just wanted so badly to believe she was going to win this battle again.

Her doctors soon pulled us aside. "You need to help her let go," they said. "She needs to know it's okay to let go."

The idea of telling someone I dearly loved that she needed to let go of the life she loved so passionately was unfathomable to me. As I tried to process what needed to be said, it was Bill who finally whispered to her, "It's okay, Jana. You can let go now. It will be all right. We will be all right."

Jana died within the hour at the age of forty-nine, with many of her closest friends and family gathered around her and holding hands. She loved living and was deeply loved by many. Although you can't ask for much more than that in life, Jana had so much more to give. I felt then how cruel and unfair life could be, even knowing in my heart that it was happening as part of a bigger plan.

My life changed immediately—how I looked at life, my drive for success and especially how I viewed my faith. I knew there was no way that the God I was raised to believe in would ever put somebody that fabulous and giving on this earth and then not accept her into heaven simply because she didn't believe or understand her higher purpose. My belief expanded. My faith no longer stopped at just believing in a higher purpose. I now knew that I would have to trust in it when it surpassed my understanding.

To me, faith is, truly, how you live your life—not what you say or learn to believe. Do you live out of love, passion and compassion for people? Do you give more than you get? Do you give in service more than you take?

Knowing Jana is now truly home, I try to let go of that haunting image of her face distorted by fear, uncertainty and anger. I hope and pray that shortly after she left this world, she found peace. The most profound lesson of Jana's loss, for me, was the fact that when she left this world, she did so without faith there was a greater purpose to this world we live in, without knowing a loving force that would protect her on her journey. It amazes me that such a loving soul would not have that strength on which to draw. I wish we could have had a deep conversation about it before she died.

Not having this conversation is my deepest regret; and yet the regret ultimately created my greatest purpose in life: to share my gifts and passions with others and to listen to and embrace the passions and gifts of others. There are so many teachers along our path. Jana was the one who taught me to surround myself with all kinds of people, friends of all ages and realms of experience from whom I could learn.

We don't know how much time we have. So take the path your heart tells you is right for you. You may not have all the answers, but nobody knows you better than you know yourself.

At twenty-seven, I got a very clear message that life was short. I knew that I wanted to leave this earth without regret, fear or uncertainty. So I made a promise to myself and to Jana that I would always live my life on purpose. I launched myself into life after college so driven that my friends and family often worry about me pushing so hard. But, I look at my drive and awareness as a huge blessing: Nobody will ever say I didn't try, that I didn't bust my butt or fail to stand back up when I got knocked down.

You will be questioned on your path. Follow your absolute core and check your gut: *Is this a good fit for me? Is this where I'm meant to be going?* We all make mistakes along the way. You're going to fail, but it's just an opportunity to say, "Okay, I probably wasn't going down the right road in the first place. I need to shift gears." Failures should never be viewed as stopping points, just lessons. Learn to take the lesson and know you will keep getting the lesson until you GET the lesson being given. We don't know how much time we have. So take the path your heart tells you is right for you. You may not have all the answers, but nobody knows you better than you know yourself.

Though she's been gone for twenty years, Jana is still my lifelong friend. She comes to me most vividly when I stumble or lose faith in my purpose. "Get moving, Sista-Friend," I say to myself, knowing Jana is watching from above. "You're not done yet."

Living her core value of being in service first, Mary Kay Sheets has been a successful, award-winning entrepreneur for more than twenty-five years. As the founder of rethink inc., Mary Kay acts as a trusted strategic business advisor to passionate entrepreneurs looking to build the functional framework necessary to operate and fund a sustainable, scalable and profitable business. Connect with Mary Kay at www.rethinkincNOW.com.

Success Is in Your DNA

Susan W. Carson, PhD

The Senior Vice President looked at me with an expression that I couldn't quite read. Was it a sneer or a smile? "Sit down, Susan," he urged. And then he hit me with it: "You will never make it in this company." My legs turned to lead. He continued: "You are a generalist, and we need people who make widgets." I felt as though I weighed a ton. It was a good thing the floor was strong; otherwise, I would have crashed right through. I heard: "Susan, you are a failure."

I had been working for this global pharmaceutical company for years, and I had always done whatever I was told to do, be it working in new products or business development. I learned new therapeutic areas whenever asked. I was a product manager when the old one was out for cancer treatment. I could do just about anything; they could put me anywhere, and I would learn the job. But, apparently, being able to do anything and communicate with anyone in the company was not a positive thing. Apparently, it meant that I wasn't good enough. My bottom fell out. Again.

My whole life I had felt that I just was not good enough. No matter how hard I tried, something was just wrong with me. I skipped two grades in school and eventually went on to get my PhD in biochemistry. I completed my post-doc and became a board-certified clinical chemist and toxicologist. But, it was not enough; it was never enough. Now, here I was again, being told *you're not good enough* by Mr. Senior VP.

My parents were survivors of the Holocaust. For them, it was not only "You're not good enough; you're not worthy" but also, "You're not worthy of survival, and we're going to kill you."

Somehow I felt that it was my job to make up for what my parents had gone through. I remember growing up in a very fearful household. And, like typical Holocaust survivors, they never talked about it.

I did learn a few things. My mom saved herself and my grandfather because she looked like a typical Aryan child—long blonde hair and big blue eyes. She came to New York on a boat, on her own, as a teenager. My father served in the Austrian army

---

That attitude of fear in our house, that was real: You can't trust anyone; you'd better make sure you're pleasing everyone.

---

before he was kicked out for being a Jew. He fled Austria when an old friend who was actually a Gestapo agent told him, "Get the hell out of here. They're coming for you next." He fought with the Resistance in Switzerland before coming to New York. My parents grew up very near each other, but did not meet until they met as survivors. I'm a first-generation American.

My parents wanted to send me to a good school, a better school than the one near Fordham Road in the Bronx, where they were sure I'd either be gunned down or knifed. So, they scrimped and saved to send me to a private girls' school. I had already skipped two grades, so I was two years younger than everyone else when I arrived. I thought there was something wrong with me because I immediately had to submit to three full days of testing. Instead of being celebrated as a bright young woman, I was told that I had to do anything I could to show I was worthy to be in that school. The sad part is I sabotaged myself in trying to prove it. I ended up being afraid of standing out, so I always tried to conform.

The message from my family was, "We don't care who you have as friends; you'll never belong." In Europe, friends would turn you in. So my parents never risked having friends again, never socialized. But, I was dying to belong to some group. In fourth grade, when all the girls were getting braces, I was so upset that I didn't need them. I hated my straight teeth: more proof that there was something wrong with me!

That attitude of fear in our house, that was real: You can't trust anyone; you'd better make sure you're pleasing everyone. Many of the beliefs that we have now, as adults, originated when we were munchkins. Some of these beliefs become hardwired. As a kid, a lot of beliefs about being unworthy, about being scared and not stepping out from myself were hardwired into me. So, when the Senior VP told me I'd never make it, that I wasn't who the company wanted, I was hardwired to take it to heart. For a few years after that I kept trying harder at what they wanted, rather than taking the hint. I did well, but was never acknowledged for it.

The great thing about that job was meeting Bill, my husband. He is not Jewish; and in old Jewish tradition, if you marry out of your faith, your parents can sit in mourning for you. My sister was

---

Each small step took me farther away from the old messages and more toward where my heart was and where I began to shine.

---

very religious too. Ultimately, I had to make the decision that being with Bill was a hell of a lot healthier than being with them and that my genuine happiness with him was and is more important than any familial problems. That was one of the most profound choices I have ever made. It started ME.

My journey to a sense of self was not over when I chose my own family or when I left that pharmaceutical job for work I truly loved as a recruiter. That VP was still in my head, joining the group that screamed, *You are not good enough!* So I kept trying harder. And the same situation repeated itself when I joined a well-established recruiting firm, where I worked hard and made the owners a lot of money. Here again was the old message. But, this time I changed the *direction* of my journey. Instead of beating my brains out trying to fit in, I started my own company and took the old one to court for the money it owed me. Each small step took me farther away from the old messages and more toward where my heart was and where I began to shine.

I'm very transparent with my son, because my job as a parent is to model things for him and empower him to be the best adult he can be. I don't remember receiving any of that kind of confidence growing up. What I remember is a lack of explanation. It wasn't

---

There is nothing wrong with my soul.
There is nothing wrong with my being.
Thank God for who I am!

---

until I was an adult that I finally had the guts to ask my father, "Why did you work seven days a week? What was wrong with me that you weren't there?" I know now that it wasn't about me. I never learned who my mother really was. She was raised a European female, almost subservient to the people around her. She was the perfect codependent. It breaks my heart.

The biggest difference in my life now is that I've grown to understand what is and what is not my authentic self. It's all about feeling totally congruent. In other words, your insides match your outsides. "This is what I believe, so this is how I behave," not, "I'm afraid to show up and be different." If your self-talk sounds like, "I feel unworthy. I don't deserve this," when you're with other people, you're going to try to show them how wonderful you are, so they'll accept you.

But, if you feel that congruence, if you want to be a part of a group, you'll simply join it. You won't have to force yourself to behave like the people around you so they'll accept you.

At that pharmaceutical firm, I thought there was something wrong with me because I could understand everybody's point of view, rather than holding fast to a single opinion of my own like the rest of the specialists. I was open to all possibilities and perspectives; I was the communication bridge perfectly suited to bring any projects together. Now, I know I have a great skill that made me a really good project manager. There is nothing wrong with my soul. There is nothing wrong with my being. Thank God for who I am!

You ever feel that sense of peace, like you're just part of the universe, part of everything? I don't mean froufrou stuff; I mean a sense of being grounded and centered. When you're trying to make yourself into something you're not, it's as though you're standing on a skateboard. You're never solid on the ground.

Your strengths are in your DNA. When you're born, you're a purely authentic person. Other people, like Mom, start telling you, "You shouldn't do this; you shouldn't do that," and over time you start incorporating it as belief, which piles on top of who you really

> *If your life isn't working, if you're stuck, it's usually because somebody put too much trash inside you.*

are. It keeps piling up—one of my clients calls it "the trash." But, that true self, your authentic self, is still there. And you can work to replace those trash beliefs, like "I'm not good enough," with beliefs that are congruent with your *real* self, the self that is in your DNA.

I liken the process of finding our authentic selves to standing in the middle of a blank stage: our parents come onto the stage with luggage, with their baggage, and they hand that baggage to us, just as their ancestors did to them. We have a choice about this baggage—and now as a coach, I try to empower people: See what works for *you*. See what works for you *now*. Change doesn't happen overnight. If it took you years to learn one way, it may take years to learn another. Keep a journal to help you track it.

If your life isn't working, if you're stuck, it's usually because somebody put too much trash inside you. God made you perfect as you emerged; your life can be much better. When you feel an itch—I don't mean the physical kind, but the kind that tells you something has to change, something isn't working—you can be the person who says, "I can see my dream. I can see where I want to be. But, how do I get to it? What's stopping me?"

The bottom line is that we have all our greatness within ourselves, despite the naysayers in the world. The truth is that your success is in your own DNA. It's all about following *your* heart, nobody else's. You don't have to do this journey alone, but your inspiration comes from the spark that is you.

SUSAN W. CARSON, PHD

Susan Carson, PhD, is a scientist, an ICF-trained coach and the founder of SMART Leadership Coaching, a firm that specializes in the development of individual leadership and communication skills for scientists and technology professionals. In the process of coaching her clients, she focuses on leading them through the transformation, which results in the life changes they seek—be it a search for life balance, career guidance or in other areas where they need assistance. To this end, Susan developed the CATALYST platform, which is designed to help them become the catalysts for the results they want using their own DNA.

Born and raised in New York City, Susan received her undergraduate degree from NYU and then went on to complete her PhD in biochemistry at Hahnemann Medical College. As a teacher at Michigan State University, she developed curriculums and lectured at both the graduate and undergraduate levels to students in medicine and medical technology. She has extensive experience in the pharmaceutical industry, having worked in business development, product marketing, clinical research and medical affairs. She has also served as a consultant to pharmaceutical and diagnostic companies. Susan's positive experience working in executive recruitment and career development led her to establish Strategic Placements, an executive recruiting firm focused on a personalized, human-centered approach to rapidly deliver harmonious partnerships between skilled executives and results-oriented enterprises. Connect with Susan at www. CatalystForResults.com.

F.L.Y.

Shaun Stephenson

"Be right back!" I called to my friend Theresa, who was waiting for me in the car. I would just grab a thing or two from the house before running back out to give Theresa a ride home.

We had just come from a women's empowerment conference, and I was so full of energy, excitement and inspiration that I practically bounced up the steps to my front door. Two years after leaving the corporate world and a six-figure salary behind to start my own business, I was broke. I had separated from my husband. And, just last week I had put my house—which was in pre-foreclosure—up for sale. Life had been anything but easy lately. But now, after the conference, I felt renewed trust in my leap of faith. After the house sold, I would start fresh, move to California and continue my journey of self-discovery.

As I opened the front door and entered the kitchen, I heard a strange hissing sound. *Where is that sound coming from? And why is it so cold in here? Did they turn off the heat?*

When I looked around and registered where the hissing was coming from, my mouth hung open, and my breath froze in the air. Everything was soaked. Huge chunks of plaster lay all over the floor where they had fallen from the ceiling, breaking cups, vases and furniture on their way down. Water pooled on the floor. The ceiling and walls were puckered and oozing. The pipes must have busted while I was away for the weekend; the whole house had flooded.

All at once, everything shattered inside. My dreams for the future crashed and burned. *Who would buy this house now?* I flipped the light switch, and nothing happened. *So, they turned off the electricity, too.*

Numbly, I picked my way through the waterlogged living room. *Why me? Why NOW? Haven't I gone through enough?* I waded into the spare room and looked up—where the ceiling should have been, I saw straight into my mom's bathroom. The adjoining porch looked like a swimming pool. My thoughts went to the water main—*I have to shut the water off!* I found a flashlight and headed

---

The pipes must have busted while I was away for the weekend; the whole house had flooded.

---

down to the basement, stepping off the last stair into about six inches of freezing, standing water, and found my way to the water main. I turned it off and headed upstairs, feeling utterly weak and hopeless. *Am I being punished? If so, for what? What do I do now?* I wished with all my heart that this would all go away as quickly as it had arrived.

Strangely, a single room on the second floor had been spared the destruction—my office, my sanctuary. It was my space, the place I went to work, meditate, write and reflect. I had covered the walls with inspiring and beautiful pictures. Sometimes I had seen the reflection of birds flying by in the surface of my glass-topped desk. All the rooms around this one had been destroyed, but as if by grace, it hadn't been touched.

Suddenly, I remembered Theresa was still in the car waiting for me. In shock, I stumbled out the door and down to the driveway. Theresa took one look at me, touched my shoulder and asked quietly, "What happened?" I burst into hot tears that burned my frozen cheeks. As I explained the disaster through my sobs, she began praying for me, holding me up and comforting me. "There is a reason for everything, Shaun," she said, "no matter how bad it looks. This is your blessing."

In that moment, it was too soon for me to see any blessing in the destruction of my life plans. My ticket to a new life had disappeared in an instant. I was broke, and I had no Plan B. I felt completely lost.

My husband and I had been friends since we were thirteen. We had always accepted and been there for each other. As I'd begun to move through my process of self-discovery, we had grown apart as partners but remained friends. And as we'd prepared to separate, I urged him to save money for a down payment on his own home. So he had recently bought a two-bedroom townhouse, and this is where I drove after dropping off Theresa—both to pick up my mom and regroup while I thought about what to do next. *Where will we go?*

How do I break the news to my family? I wondered as I drove. I was so tired and burdened, I came in and sat down without a word.

"What's going on?" my mom asked. "How was your weekend? Are you okay?"

"Mom," I replied, "I have something to tell you, but I need a minute. Or an hour. I have to just sit here and feel. Then I'll get the voice to tell you." I lay back in that chair and allowed myself to get silent. And then what Theresa said about the blessing came back to me. *Okay, God,* I thought. *I accept that you have other plans for me.*

When we walked into the house the next day, my mom and husband understood the magnitude of the devastation. We were all torn apart, but the beautiful part was that, though my husband and I were months estranged, we knew in that moment that we were still family. "Why don't you two come stay with me while we work all this out?" he said. "I wouldn't have it any other way."

Whether we're "getting along" or not, I thought, *this man will always have my back.* I humbled myself, and full of gratitude and respect, I agreed.

My mom and I stayed with him for the next year, as I wrangled with the insurance and mortgage companies. During this time, I ripped apart and rebuilt both my life and my home from the inside out.

Going through this "Titanic" moment, my home became symbolic of my life as I too was gutted, ripped apart and cleansed. *I've got to become nothing, so I can now be open and empty to build again.* I was like a clogged pipe—and I recognized that in the crisis of catharsis, whatever was in that pipe would be flushed whether I liked it or not.

During this time, I ripped apart and rebuilt both my life and my home from the inside out.

I saw into every crevice of my home, and each place represented a clogged part of my life, my beliefs, my perceptions and my fears that had been opened up.

I claimed a chair in the townhouse as my new meditation corner and stepped up my inner work with a sense of urgency. I allowed myself to feel the pain of loss. It struck me deeply that even though the rest of my home had been destroyed, my sanctuary was clean. *Yes—my center remains untouched. That's my soul, my spirit. Nothing can touch it. You can break my body, take everything I have and rip it apart, and I'll still be whole and able to grow.* Just as with the house, I was eventually able to rebuild from that one undamaged place. I had to go all the way down—to the darkest night of my soul—to uncover what I am truly made of. With that awareness, I came to a place of self-love and acceptance I had never known before.

Theresa was right. The flood *was* a blessing. That year—2009—turned out to be my best year yet. When I faced my truth and trusted I could always go within for what I needed, my life totally transformed. I discovered focus, flexibility and self-control. Opportunities came my way that turned the course of my life and guided me to what I now know was my purpose all along—to help others love themselves and access their freedom to dream. My life is such a miracle! Ultimately, the flood catapulted me from the darkness of the basement to beyond the ceiling and into the light of the whole sky.

As for the house, I went through pre-foreclosure, the flood and three loan modifications, but I still stand in my own (now rebuilt) home. Through all this, my guardian angel was my own inner resolve.

Life is about moment-by-moment learning, and I always ask to become the example of what I want to see in the world. So, now I welcome what may look like a challenge, because I know it has happened to help take me to the next level. I don't say, "Oh my God, not this again!" Instead, I say, "What am I learning? Where am I being taken in this process?" I use my challenges as stepping-stones rather than opportunities to cut off my own joy, resilience and power.

You didn't show up here by accident. You showed up ready and because you said "YES." The human evolutionary process is no different than any natural process. So, even if you are resisting

---

Through all this, my guardian angel
was my own inner resolve.

---

change, you can trust that it is necessary. When we hold onto outcomes and the desire to know how it's all going to work out, we really limit ourselves. We have to be willing to let go and surrender to what IS happening.

Transformation is not a simple process. It can be very painful. It means being dug out and ripped apart, and if you're not ready for that, you may want to give up. But, we need to feel pain and go through hardship to grow. Look at how gems and precious metals come into being—they don't look so good when they get started. Even a caterpillar turns to mush before he becomes a butterfly. Life is a process of refinement. If you think you can transform without even a flinch, you will be in for a shock. If you hold on in resistance, you will restrict what you're becoming. You're the only one who gives yourself the freedom to evolve and dream.

99

Mastery of self begins within. Where do you go for silence, for peace, for resonance or for reflection? Are you building a system? Are you learning through the dark times? Allow yourself to feel. It's part of loving and respecting yourself.

You *yourself* are sacred, your own inviolable sanctuary. That means you have whatever you need wherever you are, whatever happens. You can learn to F.L.Y. – First Love Yourself – and you will become so resolute, so resilient and so full of heart and life that nothing can ever, ever take away your freedom to dream.

Shaun Stephenson, originally from Guyana, South America, arrived in the United States on a visitor's visa in September, 1993, and acquired US residency and citizenship within a few years. From that point on, she was unencumbered in seeking her American dream. Her rise to senior client consultant with a major insurance company can only be described as meteoric, but her real passion became entrepreneurship. Today, she is an inspirational speaker, a life/spiritual coach, the founder of The Circle of Ten and Believe Your Dreams Coaching and the author of Faith vs. Fate. Shaun lives in Mantua, New Jersey with her mother Jean, to whom her book is dedicated. Connect with Shaun at www.BelieveYourDreamsCoaching.com.

Small Victories Lead to Great Triumphs

Dr. Emma Jean Thompson

Three kids pounded on our door. "Emma Jean, Emma Jean, Stink Man is beating Johnny!" I took one look at their panicky faces and raced for the playground.

Why was Stink Man fighting my brother? Everyone knew Johnny as a "peacemaker." Although he was young he had such a sense of fairness that years later he became a lawyer and the first Black judge of our city, Portsmouth, Virginia.

Stink Man was the neighborhood bully. He was only seventeen, but even the grownups were scared of him. Johnny was brave, but he was only nine years old. I was just ten myself, but I didn't worry about that. I wanted Stink Man to leave all of us kids alone. My heart thudding, I prayed, asking God for help.

What happened at the playground changed my life. Stink Man had my brother pinned to the ground and was pounding away at him. A circle of children watched, terrified, too terrified to help. Even the big kids and adults who were there seemed paralyzed by fear. But I knew, even if it hadn't been my brother being hurt, someone had to intervene.

"You get off my brother!" I shouted.

Stink Man gave me an evil grin and lifted his fist to strike Johnny again.

"Leave him alone!" I yelled, and pushed his shoulder.

"You gonna make me, Emma Jean?" Stink Man asked, glaring at me.

"Get up and see, chicken," I retorted. Oh, did that make him mad! Girl or no girl, he was about to teach me not to challenge him. But I had a secret weapon. My older brother, McKinley, had taught me judo. I prayed that God would help me to use my secret weapon well. The other kids and the adults yelled at me to run away, shocked that I was taking on the bully. But, I could see a tiny ray of hope in their eyes. And in Stink Man's eyes—a hint of fear. Finally, someone was standing up to him.

As Stink Man rushed me, time seemed to slow. He threw a punch. I ducked it; God was helping me to use what my big brother McKinley had taught me. Stink Man continued throwing punch after punch and, miraculously, I avoided each one. By now the kids

What happened at the playground
changed my life.

were giggling as Stink Man flailed at empty air. The nasty bully couldn't touch the sweet little "Bible Girl." But, this little "Bible Girl" had landed quite a few hits on him. Then, before I knew it, I took a different judo stance. Just as I'd learned from McKinley, and with the help of God, I flipped Stink Man to the ground and sat on him.

Everyone was cheering, except Stink Man. He was sobbing, embarrassed and swearing revenge.

I told him, "Behave yourself," and let him go.

Everyone continued rejoicing as he ran off crying.

God had certainly answered my prayer for help. But, I had to do more than pray. I had to be willing to stop Stink Man. I had to know what to do and I had to use that knowledge. Stopping Stink Man from bullying and terrorizing our neighborhood taught me many important life lessons. These lessons have helped me to stand up to various bullying situations. One of the most significant was years later concerning my unborn child.

I was only eleven weeks pregnant when I began bleeding profusely. My husband and I quickly made our way to the hospital, concerned for my life and our baby's life. The doctor examined me and then told me bluntly that I "passed tissue." I did not understand, so I asked him what he meant. Coldly, he said I had passed tissue and there was no baby in my uterus and that I needed an immediate D&C to prevent infection.

---

*Knowing He would never abandon me, I
waited to hear what God would say.*

"Won't that hurt the baby?" I asked.

"What baby?" he roared. "Your uterus is empty; there is no baby there."

No, that could not be true! My husband and I had prayed for a baby and finally after twelve years of marriage I was blessed to conceive.

"How can I save my baby?" I asked. "This child is an answer to prayer." But the doctor didn't want to know about that.

"Isn't there a test to prove my baby is alive?"

Fed up with my questions, the doctor said, "No, it's too early in your pregnancy. And if you don't have the D&C, you could die right here and now."

As I hesitated, the doctor became more and more angry, just like Stink Man when I told him to leave Johnny alone.

God had used me for many years to give people messages and to help them hear Him. Knowing He would never abandon me, I waited to hear what God would say. The response was instant. "Do not let that doctor touch you."

Once I heard that message, I knew I would not have the procedure that would scrape out my living baby. I would leave now, even though my blood was still flowing, and get a second opinion from another doctor tomorrow. I felt buoyed up by God's love, just as the cheering children had encouraged me on that playground so long ago.

The doctor exploded in a rage. He shoved a release form at me. "Sign this. It says I told you that you are in danger of losing your life!" When I'd signed, he barked, "You can go," and stalked off.

Through the long drive home and through that long night, every time I thought of the dangers the doctor had threatened me with, I remembered that God is faithful. I vowed to praise God even if my baby was no longer in my womb.

I got my second opinion early the next day. The new doctor told me that, though I was still bleeding, my uterus was quite thick and

*We would have our miracle
baby, our daughter Sherah.*

my cervix was closed. These were good signs. He took blood for lab tests and promised to call with the results. The next few days were an eternity.

At long last, the doctor called back. He told me my baby was alive. Through tears of joy I heard him continue, "Your baby is just fine." Soon the bleeding stopped. We would have our miracle baby, our daughter Sherah.

Our child, our sign of God's faithfulness, is grown up now. She's in graduate school, and is a true and beautiful woman of God.

Yes, God had answered my prayers for a child. And, it was up to me to act in faith. I was willing—so very willing—to bear my child. I knew I had to listen for God's message. And, once I heard it, I had to counter the doctor's anger and stand up to his bullying tactics.

Having Sherah after standing up to that angry doctor in a very scary situation made me even more determined to stand up for what is right and to stand up for everyone who cannot, or is afraid to, stand up for themselves. I am even stronger in refusing to let anyone or anything stand in the way of what God has called me to do: to champion God's purpose and dreams for other people. No matter how intimidating the obstacles, or how big and bad the bully might be, I will listen for God's message and act on it.

The Old Testament tells us about David and Goliath, the young civilian man versus the giant warrior. God didn't send David up against this huge challenge out of the blue. When David was a young lad herding sheep, a lion attacked the flock. David prayed and killed the lion with his slingshot. Then a huge bear came after the sheep. Again, David prayed and trusted the Lord, and again, he killed the beast. In the same way, my victory over the bully in the playground deepened and strengthened my trust in God, so that when I had to draw on every fiber of my faith to save my child, I could do it.

My experience as a ten-year-old child was proof of the power of faith. Each challenge I faced later in life made me more confident of God's faithfulness and more ready to face bigger challenges.

May we all move forward trusting God, knowing that God loves us no matter what we've done.

When it's the right thing to do, God will help us have the victory. And may we all recognize—no matter how tough the situation— even if we don't get the victory the way that we expect, our part is to pray and ask God for help and then do the right thing. Our doing what the Lord wants, doing the right thing in spite of fearful, threatening, scary and bullying situations is our victory. And, we can know unbelievable strength, regardless of the outcome, when we do the right thing.

Dr. Emma Jean Thompson is internationally esteemed as a speaker, #1 bestselling author (of many bestselling books), motion picture producer and trusted advisor serving leaders in ministry, business, education, entertainment and other arenas. She and her teams have been featured in various media including CNN, CSPAN, Time Magazine, USA Today, The Brian Tracy Show *and the* Michael Gerber Show. *She is the founder and CEO of MakeRoom4Jesus.com for which the Dedication Celebration was sponsored and hosted by dear family friends Dr. Nido R. and Mariana Qubein at High Point University. Dr. Emma Jean is an author in the bestselling* Get Your Woman On!

Through "Wisdom Truths" of the Holy Bible and documented success stories, Dr. Emma Jean helps you—as thousands of others have been helped—to "Make Room for Jesus" in your everyday life and, as a result, more than double your income, your free time and your peace of mind as you joyfully fulfill your God-given life purpose. As an end-time Prophet and Apostle of God and Jesus Christ, Dr. Emma Jean helps YOU profit and prosper and be in health even as YOUR soul prospers (IIIJohn2-Holy Bible). Her "Purpose Passion" is to "Cause young people and adults to be blessed in every way in this earthly life AND to be ready for the coming of Jesus Christ and Judgment Day." Connect with Dr. Emma Jean at www. MakeRoom4Jesus.com.

Thank God I Ran

Francie Kane

*H*ow far can I go? Where will I end up? I laced up the brand-new sneakers I'd saved to buy and glanced at the clock. 8:45. *All right, Francie. It doesn't matter where you end up. Just go.* I opened the door on a bright blue sunny day, took the fresh air deep into my lungs and ran out into it.

I'd never run in Fish Creek Park before. Hell, I'd never run before! But, I had to do something. I felt worthless, and I was smothering in a lifeless marriage. Seeking solace in a bottle wasn't helping. I hated the way I felt and looked, and I had to make a change or things were just going to get worse. Watching the Summer Olympics recently I had thought, *Yeah! I need to move around. I need to get healthy.* I couldn't afford a gym membership or a lot of fancy equipment, but I could afford a pair of sneakers.

The park was huge, green and rolling, with many bridges over the creek and a number of paths curving through it that I'd never even walked on, let alone run on.

Now, as I ran, exploring them was a delightful adventure. It was like driving down a street in an unfamiliar town and noticing all sorts of wonderful new things—but I was doing it all on my own, alone with nothing but my will and my middle-aged body to carry me. I felt such joy watching the morning light change as I moved through the canopy of trees, listening to the birds, seeing the squirrels dart back and forth, watching as people walked their dogs and families picnicked. Running felt like a prayer.

I ran back in my front door at 9:15. Not bad! A whole half hour! My eyes watered, my throat hurt, my legs burned and my lungs ached, but I also felt lighter, as though I'd cleared out some cobwebs. *Things are already changing. Maybe someday I'll see a way forward.* Exhausted, I stumbled to the shower and was back in the work-at-home and family routine by the time my boys got home from school.

I met Derek when I was fifteen, in the summer of 1975. I was sure, then, that it would be just a summer fling. He was twenty, and had just finished his first year in university. Being with a guy in university was thrilling and had a certain prestige. Plus, through him I had access to anything a fifteen-year-old might

---

Running felt like a prayer.

---

want, including alcohol and sex. We moved in together when I was twenty, in 1980, and from that point on, I believed I just couldn't leave. I couldn't let my parents down; I couldn't let *him* down; and I couldn't stand to be embarrassed in front of my friends. Derek and I had a friendship, and an okay relationship, but I wasn't head over heels in love with the guy. I thought about leaving a lot and then talked myself out of it.

As a young woman, I didn't know how to walk away and explore further. Then I got wrapped up in trying to please everyone but myself. So I stayed in Toronto, and Derek and I married in 1983. Fast-forward to 2000, and I was the stay-at-home mom of three kids in Calgary, Alberta. I was surrounded by a lot of people, but they really did not know *me*. My virtual business was struggling to get off the ground. My marriage was on the rocks; Derek and I had been sleeping in separate beds for years and hardly spoke. Most of our messages to each other went through the kids. While I was already in therapy, I wanted him to go with me. "We're off track. We need help. Would you go to couples therapy with me?" I asked.

He refused initially, and by the time he agreed, I had decided that he had missed his chance, and it was too late for us. I had long since taken a headlong dive straight to the bottom of a bottle and, as things deteriorated, the dive only got deeper.

I was pretending to be happy with my life, but I was deeply unsatisfied. To my husband, I hardly existed, and I pretended so well that my kids didn't know. But, I knew I wasn't being true to myself. The only time I could really express myself was when I was drunk. I was bold, then, more confident. Later, I obsessed over my destructive behavior, knowing I had to make a change but having no confidence. *I should leave and start a new life. I need to be independent, for once in my life.* I'd gone from my parents' house to Derek, and I wanted to strike out on my own and see what was possible. But, a voice in my head always piped up: *You have no skills. You're worthless. You can't do anything.*

I continued therapy on my own, without Derek. I worked on the issues surrounding my drinking. I learned about self-talk and tried to alter mine. I began to gather strength and to find ways to make myself happier and healthier. Then I began to run, and things really changed for me.

I started out with my short daily route through Fish Creek Park. I didn't measure the distance, but I always looked at the clock when I got in the door to see how long it took me. When running that loop in half an hour was no longer challenging, I pushed myself to run it in twenty-five minutes. When that wasn't satisfying anymore, I expanded the loop and found other, longer paths.

Sometimes it was a drag, and I didn't want to do it. But, most of the time it helped me. I started drinking less, so I wouldn't feel like crap while I ran. I started noticing how the voices in my head were just phantoms, trying to control me. And, every day I noticed something different and wonderful about the world. One crisp, clear morning I came face-to-face with a deer. I looked at her gentle face, her flickering ears, and felt a deep joy. "It's okay," I told her. "You take your space, and I'll take mine."

Soon, running became my medicine, a therapy I couldn't do without. I felt so free! I could cry as I ran; I could let out my emotions without being judged. So I went ahead and started to let go of years of bottled-up emotion: I screamed; I cried; I made deals with God. And then I'd look up into the sky and see hawks swooping above me.

As I ran, I thought about spiritual books I'd started reading to improve my self-esteem, like Neale Donald Walsch's *Conversations With God*. In that book, the author suggested that kinetic acts could

---

Soon, running became my medicine, a therapy I couldn't do without. I felt so free!

---

bring home a sense of self-worth and power. My favorite bridge to cross in the park had a little "1" plaque on it. I slapped it every time I came to the foot of the bridge, shouting, "I am NUMBER ONE!" with conviction.

The bridge became symbolic to me. It had a beginning, a middle and an end. I was tempted to stop in the middle, but then I would be stranded in nowhere land, sort of like where my life was. So I always pushed myself to go on to the other side. Maybe if I ran enough, I could bring my life to the other side too and finally reach independence, even though I was fearful of what was coming next. How would my children feel about the family breakup?

I had heard that athletes always "hit a wall." I honestly hated that phrase. A wall does not give or bend; it can smash both the body and the spirit of a runner. I didn't want to hit a wall! Then it dawned on me that I didn't have to. I could look at life as a portal instead. I knew intellectually I would pass through it. And though it might not be ideal on the other side, it is better than being broken by "hitting the wall." All that winter, spring, summer, fall and winter again, I ran. And gradually, as I crossed bridge after bridge, I became the opposite of broken: I was healing. I wasn't sure how it was all going to turn out, but I ALWAYS knew I would pass through that portal.

Finally, I gathered the courage to write Derek a letter asking for a divorce. "I have a lawyer," I told him. "I suggest you get one too." In December of 2002, after a series of serendipitous happenings, I found my perfect house and was able to buy it just as the divorce went through. On Super Bowl Sunday the following February, we had our first family dinner in my new house. With the eggshells finally all broken, Derek and I were finally able to relax and talk. I knew I had done the right thing!

I didn't know that I had the right to be happy. Now I have a very good life, and I feel truly content. I have a business that has grown from dabbling to success. I know I have a purpose, and I have "smarts." I'm in tune with my intuition and a much more confident

---

I didn't want to hit a wall! Then it dawned on me that I didn't have to. I could look at life as a portal instead.

---

person, and I'm thrilled to be able to nurture and support other women as they also cross life's bridges and pass through its many portals. You have to go over the bridge to get to the other side.

The work, of course, will never end. I am a lot more comfortable in my skin, but I still get nervous and deal with those issues of self-worth. But, now I'm able to slip on my butt down an icy slope, pick myself up and carry on. I may get hurt, but I know I can keep going. Thanks to Fish Creek Park, I never crashed into that wall.

You really do have the strength to cross over to the other side. It's scary, make no mistake about it; but wouldn't you rather pass through a portal than hit a wall and break your bones, or, worse, your spirit? Life may look dark, but there's a pinhole of light at the end of the tunnel. As long as you keep running toward the light, you will get through this. You WILL pass through this. There's so much beauty on the other side.

Francie Kane is the mother of three young men, a budding writer and speaker and a former membership chair of the Calgary Chapter—Canadian Association of Professional Speakers. She is also a founding member and an active supporter of the Calgary eWomen Network. In her work as a telephone expert, she is focused on B2B, outbound sales calling, appointment-setting, surveys, competitor analysis, marketing and promotion of professional speakers and virtual marketing. Francie has a knack for "De-Icing the Phone" and has made the telephone her passion. Connect with Francie at www.ProspectingBiz.com.

Bipolar and Brilliant

Vasavi Kumar

Sitting in my psychology class at Boston University, my pulse quickened as I went down the list of symptoms for mania in bipolar disorder. It was if I was reading a list about me. *Increased reckless behaviors.* Check. *Restlessness.* Check. *Sudden and extreme mood changes.* Check. *Rapid talk. Racing thoughts. Tendency toward grandiosity.* Check. Check. Check. I looked down at the list in my textbook and I knew. "That's what's wrong with me."

The realization hit me hard, but I kept on abusing my body with substances, kept on putting myself in dangerous situations, kept on going down, down, down. "What's the point in trying to take care of myself, anyway?" I rationalized. "I'm only nineteen, and I'm already f—-ed."

That summer, after I transferred to a college back home in New York, my mother took me to see a psychiatrist, hoping against hope that he would tell us my issues were easily solved, that there was nothing really wrong with me. I knew better.

When, after a series of tests he turned to my mother and said, "Your daughter is brilliant. She diagnosed herself spot on," my heart dropped into my stomach. *Bipolar disorder.* It felt so final, like I was doomed to a life of unhappiness. And in that moment, I knew for sure my deepest fear would come to pass: I would never be loved.

I wasn't surprised at the diagnosis; I always knew I was brilliant. I remember the moment I realized I was different. Every year there was a "Reflections" contest at my elementary school for second, third and fourth grade students. Each of us presented our ideas on the same topic. That year the topic was: "Does the sky have a limit?"

On my poster board I wrote, "The sky has a limit if you believe that it has a limit." The teachers were amazed that at age seven I understood this fundamental truth: that your thoughts have a

---

I always knew I was brilliant.

---

huge impact on your life. I won first prize. It was a *huge* deal; they announced me as the winner in front of the whole school. Beaming, I accepted the award, and inside I knew—*I have something special to offer.*

My jubilant mood didn't last long, however. The other kids started giving me a hard time almost immediately. They said, "Why did you win? What was so great about what you did?"

I felt so ashamed. I thought, *I must have done something wrong. I must be bad. Maybe I shouldn't shine, or let anyone see that special thing about me. If I do, other people will feel bad.* Inside I knew that I had something great inside of me, but, it was too much. I was too smart. Too energetic. Too vibrant. Too much.

From there on out, there was always a conflict. *Should I be my genius self, or should I dumb myself down just a little bit?* I covered up my genius, letting people cheat from my tests and making sure I scored lower than they so that they would feel smarter than me. It was so painful, compromising who I was, and living in that dichotomy, almost as if I was living two lives. *I am meant for more than this, but how can I act on it if other people will ridicule me for it? I'm messed up, but I'm a genius—or it's the other way around: I'm a genius, and I'm messed up.*

So I began to numb the pain. I hurt myself physically, emotionally and mentally. It didn't feel good to hurt myself in these ways, but I couldn't stop. I thought, *If I step into this genius, I will hurt a lot of people around me; they will feel less than me.* I hurt myself instead by abusing drugs and alcohol, engaging in other harmful behavior and putting myself in risky situations. I hurt myself by constantly playing small.

Even the bipolar diagnosis didn't inspire me to change. What was the point? My life was already set, my future determined. I thought, *What does it matter what I do now?* That night, after we left the psychologist's office, I went home and partied like a rock star.

Eventually, medication helped me deal with the mania, but my opinion of myself, that I should dim my light, that no one could handle my (then unfocused) brilliance, still ruled my life. And then I met Ashish.

We met at his parents' store. Tall, dark and handsome, he looked like Aladdin. I was twenty-two years old, and up until

---

I hurt myself by constantly playing small.

---

then, I had only dated "scumbags." I was not surprised to learn that in Sanskrit, the name Ashish meant "blessing." He respected me beyond belief and treated me with compassion and kindness.

He really threw me for a loop! I was uncomfortable with his treatment of me. I didn't know how to receive his kindness, and I certainly didn't think I deserved it, so I tried repeatedly to sabotage the relationship.

One night we were talking on the phone, as we did every single night, and he blurted out, "Vachi, I love you."

I said, "What did you say?" I could hear the nervousness in his voice.

"I said I love you," he replied.

I started crying hysterically. It filled me up, that he could say, "I love you" to me. I had long joked that I would "never find a guy who loves me with my hair back and my glasses on," but what I really meant was that I would never find a man who would love me for who I am—broken, wrong; a "f—ing loser." Being loved *for* me was completely out of my comfort zone because I didn't know how to love *me*.

I kept asking Ashish, "Why do you love me? Are you a fool?"

That Ashish would love me unconditionally baffled me, but it did open the door for change. For the first time since I was a child I thought, "Okay, maybe life won't be so bad." It was a slow process, but I started to consider the idea that maybe I wasn't wrong. Ashish only saw me for my greatness, and he only spoke to the best part of

---

Everything you hope to be, you already are.

---

me. I started to follow his lead and eased up on myself. I stopped forcing myself to be perfect. I took breaks, cared for myself and tried my best to love myself.

Over time, I began to see the gold in the suffering and the pain. I discovered how to focus my genius energy. The qualities on that symptoms of bipolar disorder list I had discovered so many years ago also had positive aspects. With the help of medication, prayer and unconditional love, my grandiose tendencies became big, doable dreams that I achieved almost effortlessly. My crazy energy became a drive to succeed. I went on to earn a second master's from an Ivy League school, then into an accredited training program for coaches, and finally started my own coaching business.

I learned about extremely talented people who made history who also lived with bipolar disorder, and I started to look at the label in a completely different way.

Looking back now, I see that the silver lining to bipolar disorder is that I had a gift I didn't know how to channel. Now I do.

The other day I was driving to the airport, practicing stillness. I shut off the music and imagined sitting across from myself at a table.

I asked myself, "Do you love Vasavi?"

Then I realized I didn't like that question, and so I rephrased it. "*Could* you love Vasavi?" I asked.

I looked at myself and said, "Oh, my God, I could love everything about you. You're generous and kind. You have the purest heart and soul, and you would do anything to make someone happy. You are such a beautiful human being, and I have been unkind to you for so many years."

I was overcome with tears for how much I hurt myself over the years. It was if I had taken up the role of the kids who ridiculed me when I won the "Reflections" contest in second grade, telling myself to play small. I'm still a work in progress, but I have begun to forgive myself for being unkind to myself, and that is the best place to start changing the false labels you've put on yourself. Forgive yourself *first*.

Nothing and no one can define you. Everything you hope to be, you already are. It's like the scene in *The Wizard of Oz*, when Dorothy feels as though her only hope to return to Kansas just flew away with the wizard in the hot air balloon. Glenda the Good Witch turns to her and says, "You've always had the power, my dear. You've had it all along."

I've always had the genius in me and so have you. We all have it. You don't have to be bipolar to tap into your genius; we all have the one core thing about that makes us amazing. When you ignore the hype around you, listen to yourself instead and then take action, you will shine. It's all in you—everything you need to become who you want to be, who you really are, who you *already are*. Just click your heels together three times and say, "I am meant to shine, I am meant to shine, I am meant to shine!"

Vasavi Kumar is an author, transformation expert, certified life coach and inspirational speaker. She helps clients around the world to propel their life, career and mind-body-spirit wellness to the next level and beyond. She has a particular passion for helping women entrepreneurs integrate their personal and professional success. On her weekly radio show, Deep Talk *(Sundays at 11 a.m. CST on www.710kcmo.com), Vasavi hosts conversations with world-renowned authors and thought leaders, such as Andy Dooley, John Gray, Lisa Nichols, Don Miguel Ruiz and Neale Donald Walsch.*

Vasavi holds master's degrees in special education from Hofstra University and in social work from Columbia University. She is a certified coach through Accomplishment Coaching, an International Coach Federation (ICF) accredited school. She is the author of Master the Whelm *and* S.O.U.R.C.E. *of Your Success (www.SourceOfYourSuccess.com). Connect with Vasavi at www.VasaviKumar.com.*

RECLAIMation Proclamation

Becky Skaggs

There is a quote that makes me laugh these days, although it wasn't always so funny. It was written by a woman known simply as Catherine, and goes like this: "If you can't be a good example, then you'll just have to be a horrible warning." Let my story serve you as both.

My own horrible warning came one Saturday in June a few years ago, when I awoke feeling off. My symptoms escalated throughout the day to the point where I called my doctor and told the nurse, "I think I'm having a heart attack."

It brought me no relief whatsoever when the nurse said, "I think you're having a panic attack."

I white-knuckled it through the remainder of the weekend until Monday, when I managed to get an appointment with a psychiatrist.

After I had struggled to describe the fuzzy, surreal and anxious state of mind I couldn't shake, she said, "You have general anxiety disorder and depression." Handing me prescriptions for antidepressants and Xanax, she said, "You'll be on them for the rest of your life."

I felt as though I had been punched in the chest. As dazed and confused as I was, I remember thinking, as if I knew for sure: "No, I won't."

Gratefully accepting the immediate help, I made a beeline for the nearest pharmacy. But despite the medications and my best efforts, I started on a downward spiral into paralyzing anxiety and depression for which I saw no way out.

I remember looking into the mirror one morning, something I had been avoiding for some time. When I finally caught sight of my reflection, my heart sank. *Who is this empty shell of a woman looking back at me? Where the hell has Becky gone? How did I wind up here, in someone else's life? This is not me.*

During one of my lowest points, with my husband out of town on a weekly business trip, I tuned into the latest episode of Oprah (the only thing I looked forward to) and watched Dr. Christiane

*If I was ever going to be truly well
and happy again, I needed to be on
the top of my own "to do" list.*

Northrup talk about mid-life transition and the severe symptoms and emotional upheaval that peri-menopause can cause for some women. It was as if a light bulb went on. "OMG!" I exclaimed, out loud. "I'm not going crazy—that's me!"

When the show was over, I jumped out of my impression on the couch and immediately set out for the nearest bookstore. I must have been quite a sight in my three-day-old sweats and my husband's flip-flops, but I couldn't bring myself to care. When I finally returned home to the sanctuary of the screened back porch overlooking my flower garden, I plowed through the first four chapters of *The Wisdom of Menopause* before closing the book and sitting in silence, letting it sink deep into my bones. Suddenly it all made sense, like the final click of a Rubik's Cube. If I was ever going to be truly well and happy again, I needed to be on the top of my own "to do" list.

It proved to be easier said than done, however, as many friends and family members resisted my sudden "there's a new sheriff in town" attitude. They thought that I had lost my mind and they liked me the way I was, liked things the way they were—they just didn't understand what all the fuss was about. One well-meaning friend even asked, "Why rock the boat when you're halfway through your life?"

Objectively, I could see their logic. From the outside, sure, it looked like a pretty great life—comfortable and secure. But something big was missing, and I couldn't let their fears stop me from finding out what that was. I began renegotiating some of the closest relationship contracts that were no longer working, starting with my husband. In most cases, however, my efforts fell flat. My newfound resolve was still fragile and rough around the edges, and at times I took one step forward, one sideways, and then two back. I wasn't used to asking for what I really needed; I was afraid of showing my vulnerability and being rejected.

I persevered by working on myself, spending some much-needed time being quiet enough to hear my own inner voice. Once I started listening, that quiet voice in my head wouldn't stop asking questions, each one deeper than the last. Like a runaway train, they just kept coming and wouldn't stop: *Why am I here? What is my purpose? Where is the meaning in my life?* There came a point when nothing, neither wine nor antidepressants, could silence them. My soul was no longer willing to settle for a half-lived life.

For the first time in my life I reached out and asked for HELP, and landed on my new therapist's couch in a tearful heap. When Anne told me early on that I would not only recover, but also go on to help other women do the same, I thought, "She's the one who's certifiable!" At that point, it took every ounce of strength I had simply to get dressed and take care of my family's basic needs each day. But I could tell by Anne's expression that she saw something in me—something that had been buried long ago by the obligations and duties of a life in which I twice put my own dreams on hold to get on a train and follow a husband's tracks instead of my own. When she nicknamed me "The Reclamation Project," the words gave me full-body goosebumps—this was my telltale sign that I was finally on the right set of tracks. This would not kill me.

With Anne's guidance and my own intuition, I undertook an almost archaeological excavation as I searched for the true essence of who I was at my core in order to reclaim the fractured pieces of my life. I began living more consciously, using supplements and organic food as medicine. I gave more of my time to humor, uplifting spiritual material and positive affirmations, especially when I felt that familiar panic-attack tightness in my chest and throat (as I often did).

I set aside me-time to meditate, journal and do yoga in an effort to subdue my worried thoughts. Many of my solitary nature walks ended at the Cheyenne Medicine Wheel, crying and praying for

---

This would not kill me.

---

myself and for the family and friends I didn't want to hurt and whose rejection I so deeply feared. A lot of my time was spent working through everything from my past that I had never properly acknowledged, grieved, celebrated, healed or forgiven.

Early on, when I sought out an integrative health care practice (as mentioned in the copy of *The Wisdom of Menopause* that I kept by my side like a bible), a battery of tests confirmed what I had long suspected: My hormones were off the charts and my adrenal glands were completely burned out. In addition, I began suffering from Irritable Bowel Syndrome. I knew it was due largely to the stress I had put myself under trying to take care of everyone and everything and do it perfectly, like a true baby boomer good girl.

I went about the business of reclaiming my health while also struggling with the process of identifying and eliminating the energy vampires in my life. Sadly, my marriage did not survive this process. My husband and I had become less and less connected due to challenges many mid-life couples face, and our marriage ultimately ended in an amicable divorce—at the end of the day, it wasn't great and we wanted different things. Over a friendly dinner downstairs from our mediator's office, we decided that we both wanted great.

Shortly after we sold our house, I sat down and set boundaries to reclaim the power I had unknowingly given away in exchange for love in my closest relationships. I wrote my "RECLAIMation Proclamation" to put a stake in the ground and begin living by my own set of rules. I had been a classic people-pleaser, and put my own career on hold to follow and support my husband's demanding career and to be the primary caregiver in our family.

Suddenly, I was alone and terrified, with a capital "T." I had lost all of my anchors. With my independent daughter away at college and my mom lost in the abyss of Alzheimer's, I had essentially lost my roles of mother and daughter. And now I was no longer in the role of "wife" that so identified me. I had no idea how my outdated skills would support me. There were times when I called my soon-to-be ex-husband in a panic and pleaded between choking sobs, "Please, help me get our life back." Fear of the unknown had sucked the wind out of my sails. But there was no turning back.

I got back up, dusted myself off and was proud I had stood up to her and said "NO."

For the first time in a long time, I began focusing on what really mattered to me, and what I was passionate about. With my fledgling sense of empowerment still fragile, I was careful to share my dreams only with those I knew would be supportive and took baby steps until I got my legs under me. I began to say "no" more often. There were many setbacks along the way, the worst being when I completely freaked out at esthetics school when my instructor tried to put me on the floor for the very first time with a notoriously difficult client. For the first time in months I had a full-blown panic attack, and it took a two-month medical leave for me to build my courage back up. But with the help of my RECLAIMation Proclamation, I got back up, dusted myself off and was proud I had stood up to her and said "NO."

The first part of my "RECLAIMation Proclamation" is: *To say "NO" instead of "yes" when I really mean "HELL NO,"* and the last part is: *To give my gifts and talents to the world lovingly.* When I finally became a licensed esthetician and beauty professional, I knew I had achieved the first half of my dream of helping fellow women reclaim their feminine power by becoming their most confident, beautiful mid-life selves. The second half of my dream was to become a coach, so that I could use my experience and expertise to help them on their journey—and help the men in their lives understand and support them. The transformation success stories that I have witnessed and facilitated, here in my beautiful spa retreat home, are further validation that I have found my life's true purpose.

How would *your* "RECLAIMation Proclamation" begin? How would it end? Who will you be when you live by your *own* directives, rather than those set by others? Will you rise? Will you fly? Will you reclaim the dreams that you once ran to with open arms? I hope you do. And I will be there to help you in every way I can.

Becky Skaggs is a Certified Dream Coach®, mid-life transformation coach and an esthetician and beauty professional offering individual and group coaching sessions and audio and video programs for women and men. To connect with Becky and download your own RECLAIMation Proclamation, visit www.LoveYourTransformedLife.com.

Coming Full Circle

Kelley Edelblut

For a few months, I had felt something was very wrong. My husband Pete had been acting very strangely. I noted him glued to his mobile phone, keeping odd office hours, losing a significant amount of weight, sporting a new wardrobe I'd had no part in choosing and conveniently not wearing his wedding band.

While on a family outing, my then-nine-year-old son noted a young woman stalking our family, and I noticed a car occasionally driving slowly past our house at various times of the day and night. I discovered who she was—she was the new hire in Pete's firm, his office receptionist.

Months of grieving three significant family members' deaths had left Pete distraught, and I wondered if this behavior was a related aftermath. I was frustrated; I had pleaded with him many times to get professional help, but he refused. When he left on a business trip, I called his office and found out that our stalker was also out of town. I was told that she too was traveling for business. *What business?* I thought. *Isn't she the receptionist?* I felt my heart drop—it seemed my worst suspicions might have been confirmed.

I gathered myself together and learned when Pete's flight was due to land in D.C. Then I decided to drive from my home to the airport and meet it. I called my mother and asked her to come watch my children.

"Don't ask me any questions," I told her. "I just need to go. I'll be back as soon as I can."

It was like a Lifetime movie; I went straight to the airport and literally bribed the gal at the United Airlines desk to confirm my husband's arrival gate. "I'm asking you, woman to woman," I said. "I need this."

She looked at me with compassion and said, "Go to gate D40. You've got fifteen minutes. And, sweetheart—good luck." This was before 9/11, when you could still meet someone at the gates. So, I ran to get to the next terminal and D40 in time. When I finally got there, I hid behind a pillar, my heart in my throat.

Please let me be wrong, I prayed. *He loves me. He loves our kids. He would never do this to me—he would never break up our family. Clearly, I'm insane and jumping to conclusions.*

But, of course, I was clearly *not* insane. A moment later I watched as my almost-forty-year-old husband stepped off the

---

Please let me be wrong, *I prayed.* He loves me. He loves our kids.

---

plane not alone, but with this girl from his office, who was about twenty-one. So, it was true. How surreal.

Pete and I had been together since we were seventeen. We survived professional football; we survived infertility; we'd been married almost twenty years and had two boys—we'd had a whole lifetime together. A really incredible lifetime, at that. I was devastated.

I walked up right behind them and confronted them. I ignored him for the moment and spoke to her; she acted twenty and ran away into the women's room. I followed her. "You need to leave my family alone, but most importantly my husband," I told her calmly. "He's in a really bad place and going through a lot. Stay away from him. And stay away from me and my children." When we left her in the airport, Pete got in the car, curled up and broke down—he was truly losing his mind.

Other women may not have done what I did; I could have tried to let the whole thing blow over. But, I wouldn't have been true to myself. I wouldn't have been true to my marriage and my family. Within one week, Pete moved out of our house. It was absolutely not what I wanted. I told him, "We can work through this. I know you're in bad shape—we're going to get you the help you need." Because Pete said he needed space and time to work through it and that he wanted to come home, but felt confused, we told the

---

He was fighting for his life, and I was fighting for my family.

---

kids that he was going to be working in Philadelphia for a couple of months and would be going back and forth. The agreement was that he would not see her. The fact was—he did.

We pretended everything was okay; we lived this horrific lie with our children for months until my younger son figured it out when he overheard a phone call between his dad and the other woman. The counselor said, "Your son knows. And if he knows, then he has to hear it from his father." So, Pete sat the kids down and told them.

But, I still didn't tell anyone except our immediate families, because he kept saying, "I'm working on it—" and because I knew in my heart that once I told, no one would ever accept him again.

He was fighting for his life, and I was fighting for my family. This went on for a year. When I finally knew he was never coming back, I began to tell select groups of friends. I had incredible support from all of them. His sisters, with whom I remain very close, were brave enough to say, gently, "Why do you want somebody who doesn't want you?"

I'll never forget it. I needed to hear it—but it was very hard to hear. I took a deep, shaky breath and said, "You're absolutely right."

That was terrible; but, the most devastating moment came when I realized that even though I had taken vows to be married and raise a family, I had no control over whether or not it would all end. He had been calling all the shots. And, as my children hung on to him, as I hung on, he had just been walking away and leaving us. As we fought for him, he never once fought for us. I realized that I needed to take control of my own life. I needed to figure out how to put one foot in front of the other and go forward, not backward.

I have my children to thank for that. If I hadn't had them, I would've wallowed in the pain. But, my goal was always to set a really good example for them. The kids were terrified by what they were seeing; I had to hold it together. "Boys," I told them, "All we can control is what *we* do." My low points were from nine to three, when they were in school. But, from seven to nine, their mother was on, and again from three to nine at night. As distraught as the three of us were, we were always moving forward.

I found tremendous reassurance when my decisions became all about protecting my family and moving forward. And the first thing to do was to get healthy. I had to grieve—a lot; I knew I couldn't enter a new life until I'd grieved the old, properly and

I can never say never, but I don't think I would have answered my true calling if my husband hadn't decided to end our marriage.

thoroughly, and truly experienced the loss and the pain. So, I got us all into counseling. We went for years, until we were told we didn't need it anymore, and we still go back from time to time. You never really "get over it," but you can always keep working with it.

I was in such total transition. Was I ready to date? I didn't know. Did I want a new house? I didn't know. I discovered that, in transition, you have to be open to all kinds of new experiences and people. I became the hugest marketer of myself, because I knew that Mr. Right or the right situation wasn't just going to land in my lap. I had to decide to pursue the life I wanted.

Once people saw me moving forward in a way that appeared (to them) to be pretty seamless—smile on my face, kids not missing a beat, getting my life together and even starting to date—they were calling me and saying, "Can you talk to my friend Mary?" "Can you talk to Jane?" Women in need of help started coming out of the woodwork. Not only were they calling, they called back. And, then they would call three times. I kept taking their calls. I saw that I had something to say and share, and I wanted to give back.

Somebody had been there for me, too—my dear friend Colleen, who was about a year ahead of me in the divorce process. She was instrumental in getting me through. If I could play that same role in women's lives and share everything I learned—and I learned so, so much—then I wanted to do it. I started coaching women through divorce transition, and I can't imagine a more rewarding career. Over time my practice has expanded to include many different kinds of life and career transitions. I can never say never, but I don't think I would have answered my true calling if my husband hadn't decided to end our marriage.

I see now that the low points in my life weren't actually low points; they were *turning points*. Most of us never understand why we have to take the path we take until much later. It is only then that we gain clarity about its necessity. I am grateful now for the experience, because it put me in touch with my authentic self, with my real purpose in life and with other people who live from the heart. I *was* that person that I am now coaching and helping, and I am successful because I feel accomplished and complete. I have come full circle, changing and inspiring lives, and I'm leaving a legacy for my children that we can all be proud of.

Your ending is not just an ending—it is also a beginning, full of endless possibility. It's all about your journey to a life filled with passion and purpose. What appears to be a negative experience may be that tap of destiny on your shoulder, showing you your potential and all the gifts you have to share with the world! I know now that I have truly come "full circle."

Kelley Edelblut is a certified career and life coach, a collaborative divorce coach and a Certified Highlands Assessment Affiliate. She opened Pathways to the Future in 2008 to provide professional coaching services to individuals searching for clarity in transition. Prior to her professional coaching life, she spent fifteen years in the nonprofit and corporate world in the areas of business development, marketing and sales. Kelley is happily enjoying spending time with her second husband and two sons. She volunteers with the Christ Child Society/Witts Chapter of Washington, D.C. and as a mentor to young women through Washington Women's Weekly. She recently co-founded K2A Talent Management Company. Connect with Kelley at www. PathwaysToFuture.com.

Spirit Speaks

Helen Bouldin

Hey, Love Bug. You know, every little girl dreams of meeting her Prince Charming, her soul mate and her one true love. And when I found you twenty-nine years ago, I knew I was going to live happily ever after. You were the dearest, kindest man in the world, and you are still the great guiding light and blessing in my life. My girlfriends all wanted their boyfriends or future husbands to be just like you: a man who cared, who listened, who communicated, who still opened car doors for ladies and brought them flowers.

When I found you, I couldn't believe my luck. You were an absolute dream. I loved going to see tearjerkers and chick flicks with you, traveling with you and receiving your thoughtful gifts and surprise treats. I loved holding hands with you wherever we went and having people mistake us for newlyweds when we'd been married for—fifteen years! And I loved knowing that above all, you just wanted to be where I was.

I want to tell you that I always appreciated your thoughtfulness and generosity so much. If I mentioned that my car needed gas, you would stop what you were doing, jump in the car and get it filled up with gas *and* take it through the car wash.

I would look at the price tag of a pair of designer shoes and say, "Oh my, too expensive!"

You would just smile at me and say, "Please buy them. You're worth it." Not a day went by that you didn't tell me how much you loved me and how proud you were that I agreed to marry you! I think that to other people it might seem I am embellishing, but you know it's all true.

They say that your life can change in a split second. Of course, that moment for us was when you were diagnosed with leukemia. We had just returned home from that romantic Valentine weekend in Santa Fe, New Mexico. Remember the light coming in from under the clouds and turning all the buildings a coppery pink? It was great to have that break from our business just to be together. We figured your chest congestion and shortness of breath were just

> *Not a day went by that you didn't tell me*
> *how much you loved me and how proud*
> *you were that I agreed to marry you!*

high altitude, or maybe you were catching the flu I'd just gotten over—I promise you, I really do try not to spend all my time wishing we'd gotten you to the doctor sooner.

We decided to go see the family doctor first thing on Monday morning just in case. I remember the doctor taking one look at you and saying, "You look very pale, and I'm really concerned about these symptoms. I think you should go to the ER right away and get a chest x-ray." I figured that was a good idea. The hospital could give you antibiotics too. We would be back to work in a few hours, and everything would be fine.

Of course, that was not to be. Within thirty minutes of taking a blood sample, the ER doctor told us, "Looks like leukemia." I still can't get over how nonchalant he was about it, as if he were telling us, "I think it's going to rain today."

You know me—because of my masculine emotional tendencies, I didn't break down or cry then. Instead, I immediately said, "We need to get a second opinion. We need to get more tests done. I'd better be sure to let everyone at the office know we will be out for the day." You know it's not because I didn't care—I didn't want to alarm anyone, because I truly did believe that tomorrow, we would be told that there *had* been a mistake, and you only had the flu. I didn't allow myself to think about what might be or what if; I kept focused on the immediate need. And, I didn't want you to feel any more scared than you already were.

The next morning, the oncologist confirmed the diagnosis: leukemia. And, he told us that one of the top cancer hospitals in Dallas would not provide treatment, because you did not have medical insurance. We'd had medical insurance for years! Just a few months earlier, we had allowed our policy to lapse because the premiums had doubled, and we were never sick. We had planned to replace it with another policy in January, but by then January was another world.

I couldn't believe it to be true, Honey. There was no way you were going to have anything but the best care and get well. I immediately contacted the hospital financial department to find out what our options were. I was told that to treat your leukemia, we

We would be back to work in a few hours, and everything would be fine.

were looking at a minimum thirty-day stay, and the cost would be at least $580,000. Again, the woman on the other end of the phone was as nonchalant as if she were telling me the weather report. I felt like shouting, "This is my husband you're talking about!"

I asked to speak to her supervisor, and after hours of negotiations, I got the deposit requirement reduced so you could be admitted for treatment. The hospital insisted on drafting the funds out of our bank before they would do any transfer paperwork. Then, I learned how to get insurance for you even with your pre-existing condition. The Obama administration had actually set up federally mandated medical insurance through Blue Cross Blue Shield for anyone who was denied insurance due to pre-existing conditions. But, we never had time to activate that insurance.

That same week you were approved, you passed away. You were so weak that your immune system was virtually nonexistent after being compromised by those brutal chemotherapy treatments. You were so strong and so positive, and I know you tried so hard to stay with me—you just couldn't fight off the infection.

After the nonstop activities with planning the service and hosting our family and friends, when the noise finally stopped and I was alone in our king-sized bed in the dark of the night, I was overwhelmed with sadness. I was also angry and swimming in regrets and what-ifs. What if I had insisted that you go to the doctor earlier? What if I had done a better job taking care of you? Did I tell you that I loved you every day, like you did for me? I felt so much guilt. I should have taken better care of you!

A few weeks passed of grieving, not working, worrying about the business and missing you so much I thought I might die. Then I decided to move out of Victimville. I started this written conversation with you through my journal. I'd write to ask your advice on something, like whether to put the house up for sale, and because we knew each other so well and we always communicated so beautifully, I could almost hear your voice: "Hello Love Bug… I miss you too! Just know that I am happy and everything is good. In reference to the house, you know what is best, and I will support whatever decision you make."

I know you would never think this was crazy. By writing to you, I have been able to release my pain and sadness. Over time, our conversations have become much more focused on my gratitude for you, for our great love story and for all the happy times we shared.

You would be so proud of me! I've truly metamorphosed into a strong person. You were always in front in the business, while I stayed behind the scenes playing bad cop and disciplinarian. I didn't think I could manage the business without you, but after you died, I wanted to show our employees I wasn't going to let them down. After all, fifty of them depended on us for their salaries! I turned into the first one to show up every day and the last one to leave. At first, I was afraid no one would trust my leadership—I was just "Kent's wife." But, they've seen me step up instead of give up, and they really do trust me now.

The crazy thing is, I wouldn't have learned all this if I hadn't lost you. I never would have tested myself or pushed myself out of my comfort zone and really come into my own as someone I am proud of.

The family has gotten closer, too. I always thought your kids tolerated me because I was married to their dad. But, when things did not change, when they saw me treating them the same way, being there for them, I think they realized for the first time that I

The crazy thing is, I wouldn't have learned all this if I hadn't lost you.

---

always was there for them, since they were little kids; it was always from my heart, and they were always so special to me. They didn't know that. So, they opened their hearts up to me in a whole new way. I have a stronger bond with their mom, too. She's become such a close friend; we talk almost every day now.

One of the greatest lessons I learned from you is, you reap what you sow. Now people see all sides of me—the spiritual side, the funny side and the warmhearted side. They *see Kent in me.* The other great lesson is one we lived together since the day we met— love each other today as though it's your last day. Knowing I always gave you my whole heart makes it so much easier to get out of bed each day I have to live without you.

I know nothing can bring you back, Love Bug. You were the love of my life, and I still miss you every day. But, taking the devastatingly sad experience of losing you to illness, and turning it into the blessing of knowing I can make a difference by helping others through the foundation I've created in your name, has brought immense joy back into my life. You were always so kind and giving, Honey. I know I'm making you proud.

Helen Bouldin has been an entrepreneur since the age of twenty-five. She is credited with the concept of marketing to attorneys and accountants nationwide with her Seminars At Sea program, in which clients receive their required CLE credits on board a cruise ship. In 1998, she combined her marketing and operational skills with those of her husband, Kent, and opened a manufacturing and retail custom leather furniture business. Today, The Luxury of Leather has seven retail stores in the Dallas/Fort Worth area.

In April 2011, Kent passed away from complications attributed to leukemia. In addition to operating the furniture business, Helen's current passion is launching the Kent Bouldin Foundation. Monies raised by the foundation will go toward helping individuals pay medical and other essential bills. Please visit www.KentBouldinFoundation.org and make a donation today.

In Every Setback Lies Opportunity

Anne Miner

Early Tuesday morning the phone rang. I could see from the call display that it was my favorite client, Nancy. "Good morning Nancy," I answered with a smile. There was a pause on the other end, and I just knew something was wrong. "I am so sorry, Anne. We are canceling our contract. We want you to finish up this month and then wrap up the reporting early in the New Year. It's nothing you did; we just need to eliminate the expense. I feel horrible."

I felt the color drain from my face. *Everyone in my organization works on this client's business. Without this contract, I will have to let most of them go—if not all of them. It's only three weeks before Christmas. This is awful!*

I told Nancy how much I appreciated her personal call and hung up. My husband and I had run The Dunvegan Group Ltd., helping our clients care for and retain their customers, since 1987. Losing our largest client meant ruin. *No catastrophizing, Anne.* But, no matter how hard I tried to prevent it, my bottom lip quivered when I told my husband the news.

We spent the next several days getting advice on how best to handle the employees. Each expert had a different point of view: "Lay them off now;" "Don't spoil the holiday, wait till after Christmas;" "Take back the keys;" "Change the locks;" "Revoke their login privileges." One even told me I would have to sleep in the office to protect the company's assets. I decided to trust all of my employees to behave with integrity. After all, that was a core value of the company and had served us very well for almost fifteen years. I did not change locks, take back keys or revoke login privileges. And I certainly did not sleep in the office.

It seemed most compassionate to tell the employees immediately so they could curb their Christmas spending. Everyone would be paid out their notice period and laid off indefinitely. My plan was to tell everyone as a group and then meet with each person individually to make sure they understood what was happening and answer their questions. I prepared my speech and practiced

I broke down and cried in front of all the people who were relying on me.

saying, "Everyone will be laid off—" over and over. And then, when the time came, I broke down and cried in front of all the people who were relying on me. Some of them cried too.

I was numb all the while I negotiated with the landlord for early termination of our lease, sold the office furnishings and fixtures, packed boxes of project files and organized storage.

We would try to rebuild the company by working from home. My husband set up our desks, giving us each a comfortable workspace. And there I sat, that first day, with a lump in my throat the size of a hockey puck. I had been so happy, so fulfilled, so *real* in my palatial office. We were a knowledge business, so our people were our best asset. And, now they were gone. I sat at my desk and realized: I have no revenue-producing work to do.

For weeks, I was devastated, cocooned in my loss and in my fear of the future. Since I could not talk without weeping, I decided to sit still and think. I thought about what to do. Where would we find new business? Which of our associates might be able to help us uncover opportunities—maybe even introduce us to important new contacts?

What could we do differently? How could we change our business model to reduce expenses? How could we differentiate ourselves from the competition? Some of our employees had bought their office furniture and computers from us, planning to work at home. Could they work at home for *us?* Other companies, big companies, had moved their call centers to India—could this cut our data entry costs?

I imagined what the future could look like, made notes and wrote out scenarios. Slowly, I began to see the silver lining. Here was an opportunity—to rebuild the company in a new model. I started to feel excited and energized instead of depressed and frightened. We could develop our own software and proprietary methods. We could work toward attracting clients who shared our values and valued our expertise. All we had to do was trust in possibility and our own track record.

We identified two potential outsource partners in India and decided that my husband would travel to India to meet them. I changed the voicemail greeting on our phone system to say,

*I sat at my desk and realized: I have
no revenue-producing work to do.*

"Thank you for calling the World Headquarters of The Dunvegan Group," setting the stage for growth and development into a global company. We were "open for business!"

A small *pro bono* assignment allowed us to test and adjust our new technology. Very soon, I received a call: "We heard you might have capacity to take on a new assignment. Are you interested in providing us with a proposal? You will have to compete for the job, of course."

And so we got busy preparing our proposal. It was a big assignment. We couldn't yet think about how we would re-staff, get office space and buy furniture if our proposal was accepted. We focused on winning the business—leveraging the Law of Attraction—saying out loud, "We have the best solution!"

Two other companies were short-listed. One was the biggest marketing research company in the United States; the other *thought* they were the best. The Canadian dollar was well below the American dollar. We expected to have a cost advantage. But then, two days before the presentation, we learned that we were the high bidder. We would have to rethink our presentation to focus on the value of our expertise. I bought a new suit and wrote furiously.

I had asked to be up first so we would get the committee fresh and set the standard for the other two proposals. We had one hour to present and the rest of the day to hold our breath waiting for the decision. The phone rang about 7:30 p.m. "It was a really tough decision." My heart was in my throat. "We have decided to go with—you! Congratulations!"

I breathed a huge sigh of relief. *We will be all right. Everything will work out.*

In three hectic, thrilling, glorious months, we rebuilt our company on a new, efficient model. We developed a new software application to deliver with lightning speed, giving real-time results. We invited the very best of our former employees to return (and everyone we invited agreed to return). And, soon Nancy was calling to see if we would take her company back as a client.

Within a year, we had remade the company on a remote-working model, using advanced technology to connect our valuable team members. We had our data entry completed by a company in India, which helped us deal with bottlenecks and generated a small savings. It wasn't easy. We were making our way through uncharted territory, learning on the job as some would say.

It worked! Our revenues nearly doubled from the previous year. We were at the leading edge of the technological revolution and, based on our hands-on experience, we could advise clients how best to take advantage of it. Our new clients worked with us to develop innovative solutions to their customer-retention challenges.

Equally important, under our new model, members of our team were able to respond to various family situations and continue to work from Scotland, Egypt, the Philippines, Canada and the

United States. Those who adapted to the remote model have stayed with the company for many years, providing the strength of corporate memory and trust, shortened learning curves and enhanced efficiencies.

Along the way, I had to learn to manage people differently. When you are all working together in the same office, "Management by Walking Around" works well. When people are working remotely, you cannot see them. They don't have to answer your email or your phone calls. I needed to learn to rely on people to do the right thing, to live in integrity and deliver against the promised outcomes. Trust had always been a key value in the organization—now it was the foundation of absolutely everything.

Over time, we implemented a tribal culture: a culture in which everyone works for the good of the entire tribe, making sure that our products are consistently top quality, our deadlines are met and budgets respected. We pitch in wherever and whenever

In every setback lies opportunity.

needed. We do not make people fix their weaknesses; we identify their strengths and help them get even better at what brings them satisfaction.

You might go home at the end of the day on any given day, whether it's at five, or nine or midnight and believe it just wasn't your best day. You can go one of two ways: You could allow yourself to feel frustrated and discouraged, or you could say, "Tomorrow will be a brand new day."

In every setback lies opportunity. As an entrepreneur, you will face difficulties, even disasters. When you do, set aside fear. Remember that things will always work out. You've taken the privilege of being a leader, now you must accept the responsibility and take action. Quiet your inner critic. Call up all you've learned. Rely on your core beliefs and values. There is a way through. And you can trust that, on the other side of disaster, you will find opportunities you would never realize without this challenge.

Anne Miner, BA, MBA, CMRP, is the founder and President of The Dunvegan Group Ltd., customer care and retention specialists who help companies grow by keeping satisfied customers. The Dunvegan System, and its key metric, The Dunvegan Affinity Rating™ (DAR™), have been ten years in the making and are being unveiled as the company celebrates its twenty-fifth anniversary. Anne is an entrepreneur, a visionary leader and an acknowledged expert in the field of customer satisfaction measurement. In 2008, Anne authored Measuring Up! A Guide to Success with Customer Satisfaction. *She is now developing* Speaking from Experience and Perspective, *through which she will share her experience helping others avoid pitfalls and turn disaster into opportunity.*

Anne has been active in numerous organizations and boards, including the YWCA, American Marketing Association (AMA), eWomenNetwork, National Association of Professional Women and the International Women's Forum. She is also an avid fundraiser for organizations that support women in achieving their own unique personal potentials. Connect with Anne at www.AnneMiner.com.

Safe

Kim Bernal Smith

W hen I was nineteen and hurting, I searched for something to take away the pain. Out since the age of fourteen, I had been told more than once, "You can be gay in the military—just don't tell anyone."

After a chaotic, damaging childhood, I craved the structure and security a career in the military seemed to promise. I figured, as a reservist, I could play the "Don't Ask, Don't Tell" game. However, when you have short hair and wear pants, hang around women instead of men and choose not to respond to men's advances, you get a lot of questions. As I became first an ROTC cadet and then a commissioned officer on active duty in the Air Force as a mental health professional, the questioning grew more intense. When you get caught for an "offense" like homosexuality in the military world, the consequences are severe. This happened to me not just once, but twice.

After twelve years, the military had become my whole life. And, after that many years of service, I thought I knew exactly whom to trust and when to keep my mouth shut. In Korea on a remote assignment, I got my own place off base to protect my privacy and keep my relationship secret. Still, as always, I was on everyone's radar. "Who is that friend I see you with?" people would ask. "Why aren't you married?" Though I had learned to accept it, continually having to lie and not be my true self took a daily toll. Tours in Korea are tough. Most people are there without their families for twelve months. My supervisor at the time was going through a difficult period, did not have many friends and turned to me for support as the only other female officer in our unit. We attended the same church, were both part of the choir and got along fairly well. I was told she was pretty open-minded, but I was torn and feared for my safety. *Maybe I can be there for her,* I thought. *If I find I trust her, maybe I can tell her. She is a woman, after all.*

"You can trust me, Kim," she said outright. "I'm your friend. You can tell me anything." The urge to just be myself and be accepted by her was strong. Still, I remained guarded, unwilling

---

*After twelve years, the military
had become my whole life.*

---

to confide in her and risk my career and livelihood. I had learned in childhood to always keep my mouth shut if in doubt. Then one night, toward the end of both our tours, she confided in me about her pending divorce and shared her romantic interest in a married service member.

A long silence followed this revelation. Her expectation hung in the air. *She feels exposed and wants me to confide in her, now. But is it safe?* I was stuck between a rock and a hard place. Her secret, if discovered, could get her into serious trouble. In the silence, I wrestled with a hundred different feelings. Finally, my sense of fairness and compassion, along with the desire to truly be known and accepted, won out, and I reciprocated: I told her my own secret.

Things seemed fine for about three weeks. Then, the day before I was due to leave Korea, my commander called me into his office. "You will not be leaving," he said sternly. "You are being placed on administrative hold pending the outcome of an investigation into an allegation of homosexuality."

My whole body went cold in shock and terror. Suddenly, I was lost. I had already given up my apartment, left my workplace and had my going-away party. All my personal items had been shipped back to the US, and my bags were already loaded on the plane. I had no way of knowing how long the investigation would take or how it would affect my career or my future. It was never safe to be me. Now, I knew I would trust no one.

I was told to return to work. *Return to work? Oh my God!* I had already transferred all my clients to new providers. How would I explain? The entire clinic staff was briefed about the investigation, and those who had been around during my tenure were interviewed about my alleged homosexuality. With all eyes upon me, I felt totally anxious and ashamed, and now to save my career and continue to serve my country, I had to deny all allegations. *If only someone would save me from this!* I moved in a fog, so nervous I shook constantly. I remembered the lesson I had learned in childhood and just "sucked it up."

The investigation took seven months. The Servicemembers Legal Defense Network gave me a first glimmer of hope and aided in my eventual return to full active duty. I was so surprised and

> *It was never safe to be me. Now, I knew I would trust no one.*

relieved to be cleared of the charges, I had to ask several people if it was really true. At the same time, I felt the weight of my burden settling harder on my shoulders: I would have to continue to lie. I was good at playing the game, but internally—emotionally—it was tearing me apart. I did not think I had other choices, then.

Though my life had been turned upside down, some great things came out of my "extended tour" in Korea. I found a terrific support system in my new workplace, met my life partner and got a great follow-on assignment. The next four years were the best of my career. I was always up-front and honest with my new commanders about the investigation, because I did not want them to hear about it through the grapevine. The terror, however, was not over yet. I still had not told the truth, and I still could not live openly.

I went to the meet-and-greet with my last commander, accompanied by my supervisor, with the same attitude I had had with all the others. As soon as I began my brief, I felt the temperature in the room drop about twenty degrees. My commander's eyes narrowed, and my supervisor looked rigid and afraid. We got through the briefing, but I knew something was way off. As we walked away from the meeting, my supervisor warned, "Be careful, Kim. This commander is very religious and conservative. He has such strong beliefs about homosexuality, I don't think it even matters to him that the case was cleared in your favor."

For the next two years, I walked on eggshells. My work and conduct were constantly under scrutiny. Though I was the senior mental health provider in the hospital, my commander constantly questioned my decision-making and threatened to bring in outside consultants.

Questions regarding my possible homosexuality were raised often. The self-confidence I built up in the six years previous to this assignment was gone, and depression started to leak into its place. My health suffered as I worried constantly. Unable to just be myself, I was thoroughly tired. In an effort to prove myself, I overcompensated with overwork.

Finally, my partner and I made the decision to separate from the military. We knew we could not continue to keep our relationship secret, nor did we want to. A short while before we were due to leave, I was called into the Equal Opportunity Office on allegations of sexual harassment by one of the junior officers in my command. I was floored. She had been struggling, so I tried to bond with her. As had been done frequently among the officers, I shared a dream I had with her. There was nothing sexual in the dream, the dream did not involve her and me—but it did not matter. If she felt uncomfortable, she could file a complaint.

Two months before I was scheduled to separate from the military of my own volition, I was removed from my command pending yet another investigation. At this point, I knew it did not matter. I was finished, and nothing I said or did not say would make a difference.

I started seriously questioning my value system. *Is it right to tell the truth? Or should I just keep my mouth shut?* In twenty years in the military, I had worked and worked to prove myself, and still—just as in my childhood—I could find no certainty or security. No one was going to step in and save me; I was going to have to step in and save myself.

In my twenties, I discovered in therapy that how I was raised—with great insecurity and upheaval—had had a significant impact on me. I now saw how my experiences as a child also led me to make a career choice that ultimately rejected who I was, undermining my self-esteem and self-confidence. I was always great at helping others see they had choices available to them, but was not so great at seeing that for myself. Now, I knew without a doubt I could not be a part of this abusive family anymore, in any way.

Still, it took me a year to figure out the military was not my whole identity, and it was okay to build a new one. I could be

Even if you tell yourself you're okay, the fact you have to keep a secret undermines that.

creative! I could do what I wanted with and for the people I loved! I could work on myself—not for the purpose of being accepted, but just for me. How totally freeing to finally believe in me! Now that we are free from that culture of deceit, my partner and I can finally start a family. We can raise kids who will have a much better chance of being proud of who they are and who can be proud to say they have two moms.

It was not safe to be me as a child. It was not safe to be me in the military. I was always compromising my value system because of the conflict between the vision I had for authentic relationships and my own silence. The main Air Force core value is integrity. I was trying to live up to that core value and still keep a secret, which was both damaging and impossible. As soon as I was released from that, despite all the turmoil, I was finally able to find a niche where I could support military families without those severe repercussions hanging over my head, without people judging me or devaluing me.

Even if you tell yourself you're okay, the fact you have to keep a secret undermines that. No matter the accolades you receive in life, if you do not believe in yourself and share your true self with others, the accolades will ring hollow. You are living two lives—the public and the private. Others may judge you; you do not have to listen. Only through expressing your true, authentic self and valuing yourself for who you are—as hard as that can be—will you grow into self-confidence and find peace.

Kim Bernal Smith, LISW, BCD, is known as a transformational change agent for parents. An author, speaker and advocate with expertise in the domestic violence, mental health, substance abuse, intuitive parenting and play therapy fields, Kim focuses on child empowerment and helps parents realize the true experience of why they had children in the first place. Starting her advocacy in her teens, Kim volunteered as a peer counselor for suicidal youth and for the Special Olympics. As a veteran of the Army National Guard and active-duty Air Force, and after twenty years in the military treating and advocating for military members and their families, Kim continues to support them as a consultant for the Department of Defense. She has studied with the College of Executive Coaching, is a certified professional coach, and holds licensure as a clinical social worker. Connect with Kim at www.H2HCom.com.

The Ladder of Life

Debbie Seid

"Deb, Dad's in the hospital," my sister said. "He got dizzy and fell, right on top of Mom. She took him to the clinic, but they want to do a CAT scan, so they transferred him to the hospital by ambulance."

I was really scared. My dad was ninety-five. *Could this be it? Will we lose him?* My sister said that the CAT scan results showed a significant hematoma, a blood-filled swelling in his brain. "It normally requires surgery, but we think he's too old for that," the doctor had told her.

I wanted to talk to the doctor myself, and called the hospital at 8:30 p.m. I found that Dad was again transferred, this time to the main hospital. They were doing a second CAT scan, and the doctor would call me on Monday. It was Saturday night. *Why do it tonight, if we're not going to discuss it until Monday? Dad usually goes to bed at 7:30. He must be exhausted. And why a second CAT scan?*

At 12:30 a.m., I woke to a call from the neurosurgeon. My heart clenched when I heard him say, "Your father is bleeding out of both sides of his brain. Because the hematoma is so large, we are concerned that if we do not do surgery, he may become paralyzed or go into a coma tonight." I remembered the many ways my dad had made it clear he never wanted to end up that way. He would point to older people in wheelchairs and say, "Just shoot me if I end up like that—life is for the living and that is not living."

The doctor explained that though my dad had mild dementia, he still seemed quite capable of understanding the situation and had elected to go with the surgery. "But due to the severe risks involved with performing brain surgery on an almost-ninety-six-year-old man," he went on, "I feel it is necessary to reach a consensus with your family—quickly." "Okay," I said. "I need to get ahold of my sister. I'll call you right back."

My groggy brain struggled to make sense of what was happening. My mother was asleep in the other room after taking a sleeping pill. At eighty-nine, she has significant dementia; she was

The next three days were hell.

clearly in no shape to make that kind of decision. I tried my sister, but she did not answer. Suddenly, I realized: I *am* the consensus.

I called right back and asked the doctor, "What would you do if it were *your* father?"

"Good question," he said. "Neither alternative is very hopeful at his age, I'm afraid. But I would go with the surgery, because without it, paralysis or coma is almost certain. At least with surgery, there's a fighting chance he could recover and have more time."

Shaking, I asked, "What are the risks?"

"Dying on the table," he replied; I hardly heard the host of other terrible things he told me might happen.

"Please tell me again—what did my dad say about surgery?"

"He was quite clear to go ahead with the surgery," the neurosurgeon said.

I said, "Okay, let's do it," and rushed to the hospital.

It was already 1:30 in the morning, and we had to wait two more hours before they were ready for him. Dad did his best to joke around with the doctors and nurses, but I could tell he was completely exhausted. At one point he said, "If this is going to take any longer, I may change my mind!" I felt sick to my stomach.

Part of me wanted to say, "Let's just call this off and think about it over the weekend." But then I remembered the likelihood of him becoming paralyzed or slipping into a coma overnight. I tried not to let Dad see my fear and just laughed at the jokes he kept telling.

The surgery was two-and-a-half hours long, and I spent every minute praying that he would either make a great recovery from it or simply not wake up. All I could think about was what would happen if he survived the surgery and got much worse physically or mentally. I couldn't believe that I was in the hospital waiting for him to come out of surgery when nobody else knew he had gone in. I never felt more alone in my life. At 5:30 a.m., the doctor came to me and said the surgery went very well. Dad was in recovery.

The next three days were hell. Dad was very uncomfortable and even more confused. He wasn't talking and didn't recognize any of us. He lost control of every bodily function. My sister and I were very scared that this was the end result and our dad would be in this state for the rest of his life.

Fortunately, the next day—Day 4—Dad started making progress. A physical therapist came and, with the help of a lot of equipment, Dad actually got out of bed and took a very short walk. I videotaped the event as if he were a child taking his first steps. We all laughed and clapped; I could tell my dad was extremely proud.

Days 5 and 6, unfortunately, were not as good. Dad hardly ate or drank. His cough intensified. At night he was combative and required a sitter around the clock. The nurse said that there was nothing more they could do; it was time to discharge him. I was told to get twenty-four-seven care in place by the next day.

On Day 7, Dad was brought home by ambulance. As he was transferred to the hospital bed in the living room, I looked at his wan face and felt certain he would not make it to his birthday, the very next day.

For Dad's ninety-sixth birthday on Day 8, I arranged to have a few of my friends over to celebrate with us. My dad is exceedingly outgoing and funny, and loves a crowd to entertain. Steve was the first to arrive, and he crouched down to his knees to greet my dad at eye-level. Dad's head was drooping all the way to his stomach, but when he saw Steve he looked up and asked, "Where is Patti?" (Patti is Steve's wife.) Within thirty minutes he was in his wheelchair, telling jokes. Asked how old he was, he kept saying ninety-seven. He said, "I always wanted to make it to ninety-seven, I figure I better do it this year!"

As of this writing, my dad has improved markedly. Each day he gains back more strength, and he is walking every day now, too.

We can't change what we don't see.

He talks to me on the phone often. In some ways he has actually been a bit clearer, mentally, than he was before the surgery.

Those eight terrifying, uncertain days were the most difficult of my life. What helped me get through them was what I call The Ladder of Life—the model I developed a year ago.

The Ladder of Life is designed to help people get through difficult situations and learn a completely new way of being that attracts more happiness and success to their lives. To explain the model to people, I always draw a line on a piece of paper and ask, "When things go wrong, how do you usually feel? What might you do?" People have told me they might feel angry, frustrated, scared, guilty or regretful. Sometimes they feel sad or disappointed. They may yell, blame, criticize, judge, gossip, become passive-aggressive, lie or hide. I write all of these responses below the line and identify them as "below the line" feelings and behaviors.

I ask, "If you were to respond above the line, what might you do or feel?" People say they will problem-solve, ask questions, apologize, show empathy and compassion, offer to help—basically, take responsibility! Good things happen living above the line, but the road from below to above the line is not always easy. That is where The Ladder of Life comes in.

I refer to that place below the line as "The Muck." When we get into it, we are *fighting what is.* And the more we fight, the deeper we sink. The most common word in the muck is should.

My own shoulds were: I should have made a different decision. I should have driven to my sister's house when I couldn't get her on the phone. I should have consulted my mom, or asked the doctor different questions. "Should thinking" fights what is: "It's this way, but I think it should be that way." It leads to below-the-line feelings and behavior. In my case, I was unable to focus, or to be there for my daughter. I blamed my sister for not helping enough. The Ladder of Life helps you get out of the muck.

The Ladder of Life has three steps, and the first is *Awareness*. We can't change what we don't see. Awareness is all about *seeing what is*. When I first work with a client, we spend at least a week working on awareness because being able to observe yourself is such an important life skill.

When I practice awareness, I imagine a little me on my shoulder, observing what is going on. The me on my shoulder takes it all in with lots of compassion and absolutely no judgment. When I do

---

Acceptance means accepting what is.

---

this, my mind and my body began to relax almost immediately. I become fully present to all my emotions and relax into them. When I look at what is, without judging myself, it means I am looking at myself free from my ego—a true and accurate vision. What I see is neither good nor bad, simply what is. From this state of awareness, I am ready to take the second step toward *Acceptance*.

Acceptance means *accepting what is*. To understand acceptance, it is important to understand the distinction between *Stories* (things we believe to be true, but are only based on our opinion) and *Facts* (things we can say are true and verifiable). Often, we create stories and live them as if they are facts.

Accepting what is always involves letting go of something, usually our story. Most stories produce negative feelings. My story produced guilt. To let go of the guilt, I had to let go of the story that I was to blame for my dad's condition. I had to see that it was just a story and not a fact. Letting go of stories that no longer serve is one of the most freeing experiences we can have. It's like lifting a huge, heavy cloud. The practice of seeing stories (awareness) and letting them go (acceptance) is like a muscle you develop over time. The more you use it, the stronger it gets. When I saw and let go of my story, I was free to move to the final step on the ladder: *Love*.

Love means *loving what is*—this is where the magic happens! Love is about being completely present in the moment. Love is free from ego, worrying about looking good or being right. Love is recognizing the connection we all have to each other, no matter how different we appear in the moment. Love is about compassion, generosity, gratitude and adding value in the world, every moment of every day.

Once I was able to let go of the story that I should have made a different decision, I suddenly realized that I was able to be more present with my dad and enjoy being around him whether he was having a good day or a bad one. Instead of being riddled with guilt, fear and anxiety when I see my dad struggle, I am now able to send love and healing energy his way. I am now free to experience every moment with my dad as a gift. As I sit with him on his patio, watching the wind blow through the trees, I feel a deep sense of gratitude for being alive here on this planet, in this moment in time, sharing it all with my dad.

Debbie Seid, President and founder of The Possibilities Group, is an executive and life coach with over twenty years' experience helping executives and entrepreneurs create more success and happiness in their lives. Debbie has authored many articles, models and exercises in her field, most recently The Ladder of Life. Debbie recently released The Ladder of Life Assessment, designed specifically for executives and entrepreneurs. Debbie is a certified ontological coach, and serves as faculty each year at the Global Institute for Leadership Development in Palm Desert and San Diego. Connect with Debbie at www.ThePossibilitiesGroup.com.

The Patina of Pain

Sicily Suttle-King

The orthopedist opened the door and asked, point-blank, "Do you have an oncologist already?" The terrible pain in my lower back was cancer. Immediately, everything blurred into deep, unendurable pain as I thought: *I might not be there to watch my three boys grow up.*

My pain had become so debilitating in the past year that I felt seventy-something rather than thirty-something. But, I just kept ignoring it, hoping it would get better. When the simple act of bending to pick up a saucepan threw me to my knees unable to get up, I'd known I had to do something.

But, I was not prepared for bone cancer. I was not prepared for the six months of testing at various medical facilities and a battery of specialists. And, I was certainly not prepared to die.

Many months spent at the MD Anderson Cancer Center, watching lives fade, showed me the likely reality for a patient like me. I decided to prepare myself to let it all go—up to and including the possibility of death. Physically, emotionally and spiritually exhausted, I came to the conclusion that I had no control at all over my medical situation. When I saw that, it suddenly struck me that I exerted no control over my life at all.

All these years I had deceived myself into believing I was in charge, that I could handle it all—even single-handedly fix my broken marriage. In this new light, I saw the stark reality of the controlling, jealous and oppressive behavior I'd allowed for so many years.

Old memories of his lack of trust and unfounded accusations of infidelity flooded my consciousness. I was acutely aware of the host of excuses I had concocted to support my betrayal of self: *I can deal with it. I am a good person; he will see that. I can make it better. At least, I'm getting some attention.*

I was filleted open, raw to the bone. I saw how I had worked so hard and for so many years to make it all "look good." The beautifully designed and decorated custom home with the fabulous fountain spilling into the swimming pool—what did it mean now?

I was not prepared for bone cancer.

I'd vowed to make my family and home a solid foundation for my sons, where they would feel loved and cared for. For the first time, I saw that my self-betrayal had betrayed them, too. By trying to make it all look pretty, hoping no one—especially not me—would know the truth, I had never been the mother I could have been or the mother I wanted to be.

I had been deluded by the belief that if I was good enough, complacent enough, pretty enough, accommodating enough and humble enough to never draw attention away from my insecure spouse who needed ever more validation, I would be someone of value and significance, rewarded with the love I would *finally* deserve.

I trudged through more rounds of tests, numbly going it alone because I felt safer that way. Inside was a maelstrom of chaos. The diagnosis of cancer that had metastasized to the bone was still only "probable," but I was frantic, devastated that I might not live to raise my boys. The cries that welled up from the depths of my being at that prospect could have uprooted my very foundation—if one had even existed. I knew now that I'd been living without a foundation for quite some time.

Then I was given a gift—life's greatest gifts often come in the strangest wrappings—a new diagnosis. The specialist in diseases of unknown etiology diagnosed Paget's disease of the bone—a degenerative disease that's usually found in war veterans over sixty. I had a second chance at life! And that diagnosis oddly made sense to me. Hadn't I been at war for years in my emotionally abusive marriage? Ultimately, I had been at war with myself for a long, long time. When would my tour of duty end?

My second chance was still just that: a chance. Little was known about Paget's disease of the bone. Even the doctors at MD Anderson didn't know where to send me for treatment. I was left to do as much of my own research as I could. In a bookstore's alternative health section, I grabbed Louise Hay's book on the mind-body connection, *Heal Your Body Heal Your Life*. In it, I found an alphabetical list of physical ailments, with the beliefs and thought processes that correlate with them. For instance, I

My body was reflecting exactly what I believed.

---

was awed to learn that carrying excess weight reflects the thought pattern, *I am not safe*. Your body buffers you with extra pounds when you believe something is threatening your safety.

I didn't expect the book to include Paget's, because the medical community knew so little about it. But, there it was, under the Ps. Underlying it: a feeling that "nobody cares"; you have no foundation to support you—"you have given up." A profound sense of awareness washed through me. So many times a day I had said, to myself or out loud, "It's just too hard; I give up." My body was reflecting exactly what I believed. My body wasn't lying to me, but I had been lying to myself for a very long time.

Finding that book was a miracle. My pain was a wake-up call from my soul, God and the Universe. My second chance was an opportunity to change. I was now offered the gift of a new awareness, insight into a whole new way of *being* in this world. I was not here to endure and suffer at the mercy of circumstances.

As I slowly opened my eyes to this new world, I realized that if I wanted my life to look different—and, more importantly, feel different—I had to *decide* to take responsibility and change it myself.

People put off change until the fear of living in their current circumstances is greater than the fear of making the change. Fear can be a great motivator. There is a saying, "Change is the watchword for progress." I chose change; I chose progress.

I began to read everything about spirituality I could get my hands on. I learned about the universal laws and energies that create systems and structures we can rely on: We have been given everything we need within us—a divine intelligence—to create and to be everything we are here to be. Every relationship is a call to heal the wounded parts of ourselves. We are here in this world to live our unique purpose, and to do so, we must overcome the obstacles that hold us hostage and hinder us from embracing that purpose. As I put it, we are all "Universally One, Uniquely Expressed."

As an interior designer, I use color, texture, pattern and light to transform a space. Colors had seemed muted and drab for so long, as though the world mourned with me. Now, as I resonated with new truths and energies, they lightened. I was swathed in vibrant color. Textures begged for my touch. In my new openness, I saw my clients more clearly, in their essences. The design of their exterior space began to conjoin the design and alignment of their core *interior* space, making for profound transformation. This was the most rewarding work I'd ever done, and I was inspired to earn a degree in metaphysical science.

I am grateful that I recognized I had a purpose and calling far greater than I had let myself believe in before. I honored myself—and the Universe—by finally stepping into my place of embodying my power. I now know that true power is not about force or control, but it's the relaxed sense of self that comes from knowing who you are, where you are and where you want to go. Once I claimed what was rightfully mine and let go of what wasn't, life opened up for me in ways I could have never imagined before. My sons see an example of real empowerment and joy in their mom.

We are here in accordance with the Universal Law of Advancement. Everything in this world is here to evolve. We are called to want more, do more, be more and have more. And the Universe totally supports us in every thought we choose to believe.

So, if your life and health are not reflecting expansiveness, richness and a deep sense of fulfillment in any area, heed the cry of your soul. It is telling you where you are at war within, battling against the very things you want and have been called to bring forth.

You have made a pact, and your soul is asking you to remember it. The rest of us are counting on you to fulfill that pact. When we abdicate serving ourselves, we are not serving anyone else either. And, when we are disconnected from ourselves, we are unable to genuinely connect with others.

When we abdicate serving ourselves, we are not serving anyone else either.

A patina is a natural change in surface finish that comes with age, wear and exposure. It is a richness and depth that can only come as the result of the years of repeated wear and tear. Patina adds to the value of a piece; antiques are prized for the beauty and charm of their patina.

There is a "patina of pain" that transforms the essence and quality of a person. It is the rich depth of authentic character that *only* reveals itself as we move from a place of pain to embracing the changes and transformation caused by pain. It is hard to recognize while we're going through it, but pain is truly a transformative gift. If you use it to become new, whole and vibrant, what is ultimately revealed is a woman of distinction; a woman of substance, living her art.

Oh, Paget's disease of the bone, that debilitating, degenerative disease the doctors didn't know how to treat? It's gone. It simply disappeared. The doctors can find no trace of it. When your soul finally gets your attention, the condition that shouted at you is no longer needed.

Sicily Suttle-King is the founder of Epoche' Living, a holistic lifestyle design company, and sister company, Epoche' Studio, offering a myriad of experiences intended to mentor women in designing styles of living that liberate their innate, yet hidden power. Sicily's work is best described as an intuitive visionary balance and refinement of aesthetic and energetic properties from "soul code to zip code." With an MS in metaphysical science, she is a highly sought-after speaker, life coach, designer and consultant.

Sicily has been a top-producing territory sales manager in the luxury home design market and has been a product design consultant for home décor manufacturers. She has owned her own successful interior-design firm. Based in Austin, Texas, Sicily also creates and facilitates life skills workshops for domestically abused women and is currently working toward her PhD. Connect with Sicily at www.EpocheLiving.com and www. EpocheStudio.com.

At the Foot of the Mountain

Joy Golliver

I *am really going to lose Bob. He is going to die!*

Since the news—my husband's 2001 diagnosis of Alzheimer's disease—I'd done a lot of reading. All the research said there was no cure, that Alzheimer's was terminal and we'd have about ten years at best. As a take-charge person, I was used to being able to control my life. I thought there must be an answer. *There must be a new pill, a new research program, some magic cure—there must be something*, I told myself. *I'll find it.*

Now, home from an appointment with the neurologist, the news of Bob's ever-lower cognitive test scores sinks in, and I sit down and cry. After hoping to find an answer for two years, I finally have to admit the truth: *There is no answer. There is no cure. I can't fix it, not with all my skills and talents and love. This is going to be our life.*

Bob and I were high school sweethearts. Bob lettered in tennis and swimming; yet, he was always in trouble for talking back to the teachers. I was the opposite: very involved in my church and getting good grades. For years, when we would go back to our reunions, the principal told us he never thought our marriage would work.

Opposites do attract, and we were happily married best friends for fifty-five years. Bob was one of the smartest people I ever met. After we were married, he earned degrees in both law and engineering. He had been President of Washington Natural Gas, a company with over a thousand employees.

About a year before his diagnosis, I started to suspect that Bob was experiencing some form of dementia. He had always had a very sharp mind, and now I saw him search for words. Then, one day I found the ice cream in the kitchen cabinet.

At first, I couldn't get his doctor to talk to me about my concerns because of privacy rules. But, when I took Bob to the doctor after a fall, and Bob asked me to come into the examination room with him, it finally became apparent to the doctor that something wasn't normal. Bob kept turning around, waiting for me to supply all the answers. After tests, the diagnosis was made. I remained in denial

---

Then, one day I found the ice cream in the kitchen cabinet.

---

for many years, holding the hope that I could somehow fix Bob's disease and our rapidly changing lives.

While Bob was President at the utility company, I had my own business for twelve years. We often traveled together for his work or mine. Over time, we traveled less and less, and after the grief and shock abated a little, I accepted that it didn't make sense for Bob to travel anymore. In fact, though I loved my work, it no longer made sense for me to try to run a business either. We were very lucky I was not the breadwinner of the family and that we were financially secure. Being Bob's caregiver became my full-time job.

Caregiving was anything but easy. It was devastating to watch Bob deteriorate, and I often felt as though my life was on hold. I missed having my business. I felt lonely and frustrated. I decided I would not spend the time we had together being negative. I would make it as positive an experience as I could and find all kinds of ways for us to really enjoy our time together, living in the present *and* reliving all of our happy memories.

We loved to laugh together. We used to take drives together, down the same route so Bob would know where we were. There were funny little things along the route that we'd laugh at, like a gigantic metal turtle sculpture Bob named Gus—after his best friend. Every time we passed it, I'd say, "Bob, there's Gus!" and we would laugh.

At Bob's first cognitive MIME test appointment with the neurologist, the doctor touched his collar and asked, "What's this?"

"Your collar," Bob answered.

The doctor pulled at the cuff of his shirt. "What's this?"

Bob answered, "Your cuff."

"What's this?" The doctor pulled on his necktie.

"That's a damned ugly tie!" Bob said. We all laughed. He made that joke every time the doctor did the test. For years, when he couldn't identify a collar or cuff, he still remembered his joke and made everyone laugh.

All caregivers get frustrated, angry and impatient. Sometimes I just wanted to scream—"I want to be normal, like other people!" I developed many tools for coping and self-care. One of the best was the time-out. Sometimes I would take a mini time-out and just go sit in the bathroom. It was decorated to resemble a garden. At other times, I would get someone to stay with Bob while I took

---

Sometimes I would take a mini time-out and just go sit in the bathroom.

---

a four-hour Me Day and went to a hotel. To sit around the pool, read and drink a latte was bliss. I'd go through the shops, sit by the fountains and notice who was in the convention end of the hotel. I wasn't just a caregiver; I was a normal person in a beautiful world. That little bit of heaven refreshed me enough that I could go back to my job.

A point came when the physical demands of caregiving were too much for me. After I moved Bob into a skilled nursing facility in 2009, I had a major crash. I thought that the move would reduce stress, but I missed him terribly, and it was hard to turn over my loved one to a facility with its own protocols. The answer to every question I asked was, "Well, these are the rules. We can't have special little needs for every patient." After Bob fell seven times in the first eight weeks, I woke up at three in the morning sobbing uncontrollably.

Three hours later, I still lay there sobbing, saying to myself, *Joy, you're in trouble. You've got to get help.*

I had a small support team in place, but I couldn't get out of bed to call them. Finally, I willed myself to get off the bed and onto the floor. I crawled to the bathroom, splashed water on my face and made my calls. My friends and daughter came and saved me. They decided that I could not go to see Bob for a while. They

---

If you don't have a plan, you'll crash.

---

would take over visiting and dealing with the facility for at least a week. I promised to eat three times a day, and they arranged to have my evening meal brought to me. And every day I had to leave my apartment, go out into the world, sit in one of my quiet spaces and write.

I knew that I needed to write in my journal, because my stomach hurt so badly. I went to Starbucks for a quick latte and oatmeal. My journal was open in front of me as I drank my coffee, and when I "came to" I had written thirty pages about all that I had learned as a caregiver. Eventually, those thirty pages became a published booklet: *Self Care for Caregivers: 161 Tips to Make Your Life Easier.* From then on, when a crash came, or a very stressful day, I went to my journal and poured out all the anger. I had to get it out of my system: everything I was mad about, everything that was eating my soul. Once I dumped it all in my journal, God began to heal me. Then, I was able to move on.

There are so many gifts in the experience if you look for them. I kept a gratitude journal and recorded what I was grateful for every day. It is filled with the joyful, happy experiences Bob and I enjoyed along the journey. This was one of the many tools I used to take control of what I *could* control. And that made me believe that, come what may, I could handle the biggest challenge of my life. I could relax a bit. We could laugh together, enjoy our music and dance around the living room. We learned to enjoy every moment, noticing new flowers in bloom or a full moon in the dark sky.

In 2009, Bob lost his ability to speak. He lost all verbal communication. We learned to connect soul to soul. I could talk to him, of course, and he could answer with little sounds. He got to talking with his eyebrows—he would wiggle his eyebrows and smile or frown. That's why, though I'm not certain, I think Bob understood more than we might have guessed. We were so connected; I think he knew me up until the very end.

After Bob passed away in February, 2010, I hit another wall while I tried to move on. *Who am I? Who do I want to be?* I had cared for Bob for ten years through the good times and bad, through laughter and tears, hospice and death. I felt a deep sense

If you want to climb Mount Everest, you don't stand at the foot of the mountain unprepared.

of loss at the death of my husband. But, we had discovered the deepest love, companionship and commitment. *Could I reinvent myself again at seventy-five?* I heard God's voice loud and clear: "You know the answer." Suddenly, a line I had written came back to me: "One person can make a difference, and together we can change the world." Touched By Joy was born. The mission: Celebrate, educate, validate and empower caregivers around the world.

In this era of aging baby boomers, almost all of us will face a challenge related to illness in our lives, be it temporary or terminal. You need to be prepared in advance for anything that *might* happen, so you won't be thrown for a loop when it does. If you don't have a plan, you'll crash. If you have already thought it through, it won't take you down. A part of succeeding in your business is being prepared for illness or a financial setback. We tend to ignore these issues, because we don't want to face them.

Go through a list of questions. What could you do as a business owner to prepare to handle illness? What would happen if you were the patient? Do you have a plan? Do you have a plan if you need to become a caregiver to a parent and have to add this to your current workload? Now is the right time to have a family meeting and say, "I want to make sure I have all the information I need from you. Let's think now about what your wishes are." Most people I talk to admit they're already afraid of what might happen—why not prepare for anything and ease the worry and the fear?

Prepare for everything, including success as you define it. I define it as being ready for the inevitable or the unavoidable. For example: as a caregiver, when I realized I had no control over what might happen, I decided to address caregiving as a business, because I knew how to do that! When it became a creative process and I started coming up with tips, tools and resources to make my life easier, I knew I had my plan in place. When I reached each stage with Bob, I was prepared. If you want to climb Mount Everest, you don't stand at the foot of the mountain unprepared.

Preparation also allowed me the freedom to take really good care of myself. As Dr. Phil said to the married women in his audience, "If you really love your spouse, you should take really good care of his wife." The same holds true if we care for a child, wife or parent. If we allow ourselves to get sick, who will take care of our loved one? We owe it to them and to ourselves to stay healthy and whole. You absolutely must take time-outs to do what feeds your soul. In order to save ourselves, we have to learn to use stress-releasing tools and tips. That is what I did, and that is what I teach.

166

Joy Golliver is the founder of Touched By Joy, Self Care for Caregivers, and Ignite the Community Spirit. Joy gives keynote speeches and workshops for caregivers. She has written several books: Self Care for Caregivers: The Most Important Person in the Experience is YOU!; Self Care for Caregivers: 161 Tips to Make Your Life Easier; Ignite the Community Spirit: 300 Creative Ideas for Community Involvement; *and* I CAN Ignite The Community Spirit: 301 Ways to Turn Caring Into Action! *Her* I CAN *newsletter has been distributed free to volunteer conferences around the United States. Joy is currently writing her life story,* The Involuntary Caregiver. *Connect with her at www.TouchedByJoy.com or www.JoyGolliver.com.*

Life after Death

Beverly Trujillo Grover

On October 2nd, 2005, a sunny Sunday afternoon, Tim—my husband of twenty-one years—left for Chile. We had just arrived in Reno, Nevada having taken an inspiring nine-day road trip from our previous home in Fairbanks, Alaska through the glorious redwoods of Northern California.

Tim had been transferred to Reno with his job. We were so excited for our new life to begin! The company Tim worked for had asked him to make a trip to Chile. Tim, always the dependable one, agreed, even though our daughter Annie was due to deliver her first baby the following week.

I said goodbye to him at the curb as he walked into the terminal and turned around to smile and blow me a kiss goodbye.

Even as I drove away from the airport, having just dropped him off, all I could think about was Tim's return. We had so much to look forward to: relocating from Fairbanks; moving into the new home that we had just purchased; seeing all of our children; and welcoming another grandchild into the world. I traveled to California, where my daughter Annie and I enjoyed three wonderful days doing all the things you do to prepare for the arrival of a new baby.

Unable to track me down in California, the company called my son Derek first. Then he called me. At his first words, "Mom, I need you to sit down," my heart seemed to stop. Everything blurred. "Dad passed away in Chile today, Mom. He's gone." It was like a bomb going off. My entire world exploded.

I gave the phone to my daughter, my mind racing with pleading thoughts and prayers. *No! Tim can't be gone! We have so many things to do! God, please don't take my best friend, the love of my life, my soulmate. Please, God!* I collapsed into a chair, face in hands, and wondered, *Am I dreaming?*

I kept replaying our last moments at the airport over and over again, seeing his face. In the distance I could hear my daughter vomiting and sobbing in the bathroom and I knew our lives would never be the same.

That night was the longest night of my life. My heart was in such great pain, and all my thoughts were of Tim's final moments. *Where was he when he died? Did he know what was happening to*

It was like a bomb going off. My entire world exploded.

---

him? Was he scared? Images from our many years together ran rapidly through my mind, and all my lifeless body could manage to do was cry and cry. *Tim, what will I do without you?*

Everything just bled into everything else after that: my relocation to Reno, the funeral, the birth of Annie's child and time itself. Those moments that should have been filled with joy were continually punctured by our grief. My children and I would go from laughing to breaking down into tears, holding each other, trying to let our shared sorrow somehow make it all better. But it didn't.

When I saw Tim lying there still and silent in the casket, it suddenly hit me: I would never be with him ever again. We would never hold each other, never kiss each other, never spend time enjoying each other and our little family; he would never get to play with his grandchildren. My children thought I would die of a broken heart, and so did I. Who was I now, without Tim? A widow?

170

What was that? I now had to be everything for my children and myself; all I wanted to do was run.

I couldn't stay in my own home. I was always looking for reasons to leave my home and be with other people. I couldn't bring myself to go through Tim's things. I cried all the time. My body began to shut down. I looked for him at restaurants, around corners; it was too much.

A constant prayer played over and over in my head and I clung to it as if it were a rock in a rushing river: *Lord, help me to remember there is nothing that will happen today that you and I can't handle together.* But even as I spoke those words, I wondered if I would truly be able to handle it.

The first Christmas after his death I drove around trying to take care of all those holiday errands a mother has to take care of, and found myself stopping in a parking lot to call Tim from my cell phone and ask him which presents we should get for our kids. Then I suddenly realized what I was doing. It was a horrific moment. I have never felt more alone, more lost.

---

*It just did not seem possible that
Tim wasn't coming home.*

It just did not seem possible that Tim wasn't coming home. I kept expecting him to walk through the front door to hug me, to kiss me and tell me it had all been a horrible nightmare. But he didn't. I offered it up to God, praying as hard as I could, losing myself in my work, making sure my children were okay and reminding myself that the Lord only presents us with challenges that we can handle, but this seemed more than I could cope with: relocating to a new city, purchasing a new home, burying my husband and welcoming a new granddaughter.

My first turning point came in the summer of 2008, at my daughter's wedding. My son Derek had been compiling a video taken from footage of Tim and Annie while she was growing up. He was going to show it during the father/daughter dance at the wedding. We all helped Derek go through the footage, edit the compilation and score it to the beautiful song, "Because You Loved Me." Somehow, sitting through those memories—those moving images flashing on the screen—helped us come together as a family and process our feelings as a family; it helped us begin healing as a family.

The wedding ceremony and reception took place at a vineyard, under the open sky. Annie was still devastated that Tim could not walk her down the aisle, telling me through her tears that she couldn't believe he wasn't there, that he wasn't going to be part of it. I found the strength to tell her what he would have said: "Time to get tough, honey!"

He would have wanted us to enjoy this special day. And we did. During the ceremony we all noticed a glorious bald eagle soaring above us, circling and circling. Only when Annie got into her carriage and drove away did the eagle fly off. To this day I believe that that eagle was Tim's spirit, hovering over us. He never missed his children's events. Ever. And as I watched Annie's brothers take turns dancing with her during the father-daughter dance, the images from the video playing on the screen, it was as if he really *was* there.

Driving home after the wedding weekend, I began to feel a new strength grow inside me. All this time I had been asking God, *Why? Why me? This is more than I can handle! Please bring back my husband! How can I possibly go on without him?* But now this new strength, this new voice—perhaps it was Tim's voice—had something new to offer. It said, "Just start living for yourself, Bev. Go back to what you love. Enjoy your life to the fullest. Only you can do it."

I realized then that the only answer was to try to be the kind of person Tim had always known me to be. I learned how to travel by myself. I learned to love and take pride in my home again. I learned how to play with my grandchildren. I began to cherish and enjoy my children again. But mostly I learned how to love myself again.

I turned my life over to God and His message to me was loud and clear: "You can and you will!" I stopped asking him, "Why?" and started living again. I knew He would take me to the next level. I believe everything good happens to those who "do good." Things happen for a reason, even death and loss.

Learning to live again meant learning how to go back to what I loved. I began sewing, crocheting and gardening. I learned how to enjoy my new journey of experiencing life alone. I began growing again. I spent more time with my wonderful mother, who

> *I allowed myself to enjoy everyone again—*
> *my mother, my children, my grandchildren.*
> *The way to honor Tim was to live.*

had been my rock during the time of Tim's passing, telling her, "I now know the key was to learn how to move on in God's will." I allowed myself to enjoy everyone again—my mother, my children, my grandchildren. The way to honor Tim was to live.

Over the last six years I have experienced incredible changes in my life. Six months after my husband passed, I went to work as an administrative assistant and later became an insurance agent, as I believe passionately that people need to protect their families when tragedies occur. My ultimate plan, with the help of God, will be to start a business where I can help people deal with their life-changing situations as a Christian life coach. I want to help guide them through the pain I felt.

I continue to take online classes and plan to bring this dream into actuality in the very near future, God willing. I may not have all the answers for those experiencing similar tragedies, but I know that I have the heart, the compassion, the will and the knowledge that they too can grow in the same way I have.

My children and I talk of Tim often. We loved him so much, and we never thought we'd have to live without him. We appreciate everything. We love to the extent of our hearts. Our success lies in gratitude, connection and appreciation of every little beautiful thing. Success is being in a valley so low, yet knowing we are not going to stay there. We succeeded, surviving the loss of someone we loved dearly, someone we depended on and someone who always brought us together. We continue to live the life Tim would have expected us to live.

Life can change in a blink of an eye—it doesn't matter what you have planned. God has a plan for our lives; His plan is the one we have to accept. Love those who mean the most to you. Spend every moment possible cherishing those who are an important part of your life. There *is* Life after Death. It is love.

Beverly Trujillo Grover, wife of beloved husband Timothy Raymond Grover for twenty-one years and mother to four children and six grandchildren, worked for fifteen years as an administrative assistant for the mining industry. Currently an office administrator in a life/health insurance broker's office, Beverly is a member of the outreach group of Summit Christian Church, current president of the Sierra Reno chapter of Business Networking International and a proud member of the eWomenNetwork. Connect with Beverly at www.Inspired-Hope.com.

All Your Issues Are in Your Tissues

Carole M. Friesen

I'm standing frozen in the front of the room, facing the twelve other students and our instructor, fighting a tremendous energy rising inside of me. *What's going on? Where is all this energy coming from? I'm pouring sweat. Why the hell did I sign up for this course?*

I have just spent the last two days with a partner, reading each other's bodies in our underwear. I am supposed to write a report on what I discovered from her BodyMind Analysis.

As the minutes tick by, I freeze. I can't write a word. Not a single word. *WOW!* As I stare at the blank piece of paper, the energy within me gets harder and harder to suppress. I only have a half an hour. Tick tock, tick tock… only fifteen minutes left. *Oh my God! Only fifteen minutes to finish before I have to read this in front of the whole group.* I can't write anything. Nothing. My body is numb. Now I am fighting back the tears. My brain is going a million miles an hour. I'm fighting something. It's as if my soul is telling me: "There is something we haven't dealt with, and we are going to deal with it right now."

In front of everyone, I feel something snapping inside of me, like thousands of rubber bands breaking all at once. As my body releases, I am brought whirling back to the moment when my power was taken away from me, the moment when I began to armor myself emotionally and physically. In that moment, I finally cry out thirty-eight long years of pent-up anger, pain, grief, guilt and humiliation.

The year I entered second grade, we moved three times. I attended a small two-room country school with six grades in one room. During a spelling test one morning, Janet, the girl beside me, was talking to me. As I was telling her to be quiet, the teacher saw me talking and accused me of cheating, in front of everyone. He marched over, grabbed me by the collar and hauled me into the back room. He told me to put out my hand and hit me hard with a leather strap.

Walking out of that room and back into the classroom, I felt the sting of humiliation much more than the throbbing pain in

---

It's as if my soul is telling me: "There is something we haven't dealt with, and we are going to deal with it right now."

---

my hand. All day I worried about telling my parents what had happened, and when I did, the whole family teased me. I was devastated. From then on, I hated English, and I put up a wall between myself and that experience. I vowed that no one would ever hurt that beautiful, vulnerable little girl again.

We moved again, into a bigger community, and my reputation for being a poor reader and speller placed me at the back of the classroom with all the so-called dunces. Any time I was asked to answer a question or read out loud, things went blurry. I told my teachers: "I can't see the blackboard." Then I needed glasses. One of my friends corrected all my homework for me. She checked my spelling and grammar in every assignment. She had my back. I was one of seven children, and no one had the extra time to work with me. Nobody encouraged or helped me—they just thought I was dumb. So I went through school and most of my adult life believing that I was half stupid, even though I got As and Bs in every subject except English. This vulnerability tripped me up every day of my life and slowly chipped away at my self-confidence.

So many situations required me to write and spell. I kept reinforcing my belief: *I can't do this!* I was terrified of speaking in public. I started gaining weight. I became the class clown, the tomboy no one could hurt. My dream was to be a nurse, and I was turned down due to bad marks in English.

The masculine energy that protected me as a tomboy continued to serve me in my adult life. I owned and operated a successful bistro and blues bar for fourteen years. Even though I could do it all, my insecurities crept in: I never held a staff meeting; I never once took my own stage; and I hired someone to take care of my correspondence. I wore black, tied my hair in a tight bun and told my employees, "Leave your damn emotions at home! We've got beer to sling." I thought I was in charge, but I was only in control.

In 2000, a year after selling my business, I realized I wanted something more from life. I decided to do some inner work. I signed up for the workshop that changed my life: "The Magic of BodyMind Communication." I thought I had mentally dealt with all the pain, yet here I was, suppressing years of pent-up hurt. I

This vulnerability tripped me up every day of my life and slowly chipped away at my self-confidence.

hadn't realized that I had stored that early experience in my cellular memory. I hadn't realized how many times it tripped me up in my adult life. Hiding my insecurities took a tremendous amount of energy. In the moment when I released it, it all unraveled and freed my body. My body surged with an energy I had never felt before.

In the days and weeks that followed, the whole world changed for me. I took a different direction—the direction of self-love. I was in ecstasy! It was like having a full-body orgasm that lasted for weeks! Ever since that day at the workshop, I have been able to spell just fine, and now I love public speaking.

I had totally lived in my head; I didn't even know I had a body. I just dragged the poor thing along. Suddenly, I was present, listening to my body. I now perceive things differently. I learned how to stand in my power, fully activated and in charge. Insecurities no longer haunt me. They had all originated where I had been wounded so long ago, and I started to feel freedom and empowerment by letting them go. I now accept and love myself exactly as I am, instead of how I thought the world wanted me to be.

Now I understand how the BodyMind works at protecting that vulnerable little child in all of us. I discovered that I am a walking

*I thought I was in charge, but
I was only in control.*

autobiography of my life. My life experiences show in every part of my physical body. My body has all the wisdom! My weight was my body's way of protecting my innermost feelings; my back pain was the tension I felt from busting my back to please others. Wow! Talk about coming home to myself: I came home to an understanding that my beautiful body only wanted my love and acceptance. Other people started seeing me differently, too! I released twenty pounds of protection, and my whole face softened from letting go of all those suppressed emotions.

Every incident or accident that happened in my life was related to power. Our power is in the stomach area; we process it through the solar plexus. The strap on the hand in second grade actually hit me bang in the solar plexus. So, it took away my power; but when I took it back, it was using my feminine energy, not the masculine energy I used for so long to protect my vulnerability. I discovered that my softness, gentleness and my juicy female body are where my real power comes from.

Letting go of cellular memory is like turning the light on in a dark, dusty corner. All the spiders and nasty things scurry, the cobwebs clear out. You begin to glow. Your body has all the wisdom. You can read a thousand books about how to ride a bicycle, but until you actually get on one, you don't fully understand it. The same is true with your issues. All your issues are in your tissues!

I really believe that the universe set me up for this beautiful journey, and that I needed all these challenges—or what I call fertilizer—to grow and find my path. It's in our challenges that we find our growth; otherwise we stay just the same. Finding the diamonds in the dog shit made me who I am today. You can succeed in spite of your challenges when you seek out the diamond, the one little gift in each challenge. And once you learn from that experience, you can let it go.

No longer afraid to step onto my own stage, I have been in service to the work that changed my life for many years. I teach the same course in BodyMind Communication that first opened me up to my own story. I am a keynote speaker all over North America. I am a face reader and a fluent speaker of the most expressive language of all: the body's language. I have empowered thousands of people to come home to themselves by understanding and loving the autobiographies of their own bodies.

All your stories are inside you. Your journey to empowerment is in your own beautiful body, and if you are in your body, aware and present, you too can achieve your own success. Your body is the vehicle on this journey, so get in the driver's seat!

ALL YOUR ISSUES ARE IN YOUR TISSUES

A sought-after keynote speaker and an award-winning teacher with a diploma in psychosomatic therapy, Carole M. Friesen is in the business of empowerment. Through self-awareness, she shares how to peel back the emotional layers of cellular memory and discover that true power is within. Carole is the North American spokesperson for the Australasian Institute of BodyMind Analysis and Psychosomatic Therapy and oversees thousands of students, practitioners and teachers in psychosomatic therapy. Carole has worked closely with the Founder and Director of the institute, Hermann Müller, since 2001. She has shared the stage with New York bestselling authors T. Harv Eker, John Gray and Doreen Virtue. Spend a few minutes in Carole's presence and feel your body come alive! Connect with Carole at www.PsychosomaticTherapy.com.

Finding Me

Johnell Borer McCauley

"Call the paramedics." My mother's voice on the phone startled me. We had been chatting just moments before, planning a Valentine's Day lunch for my sister Mary and her daughter, who were flying in to visit. What could have happened in the past few minutes that required the paramedics?

"I fell. My head..." Mom tried to explain. I hung up and called the paramedics, and then rushed to her house. I was beyond worried. She had been diagnosed with stage four cancer several years before, but continued to amaze her doctors with her will to live. The disease had taken a toll, however. *Would she be okay? Was she strong enough to handle the effects of the fall?*

I took comfort in the knowledge that my mom was a fighter. In addition to cancer, she had also survived polio as a young adult. And, even after doctors told her she wasn't strong enough to handle a single pregnancy, she had given birth to nine healthy children.

Mom was alert when we arrived at the hospital, but she deteriorated rapidly. The doctors quickly realized that she would need surgery to correct the damage caused by her head injury. I was so relieved when she came out of surgery, but my relief was fleeting. It soon became clear that her body, weakened by years of cancer and challenging treatments, simply could not handle any more.

Within thirty-six hours, my whole world was torn apart. My mom, my best friend, my mentor, was gone. I knew for certain that my life would never be the same again. During the fifteen years since my father had passed away, my mom and I became very close. We spoke every day. We shared so many wonderful memories together roaming the bead stores, shopping, cooking, drinking a glass of wine. We'd talk about anything and everything—our

> *Within thirty-six hours, my whole world was torn apart.*

kids, our purpose in life, the future. Every day on my drive home from work, I would put in my Bluetooth and call Mom. We'd talk and talk, catching up on the family, the news, what she did that day. She always knew when I was home—even over the phone, she could hear my garage door open. It was her cue to say goodnight.

In the weeks after her death I was so preoccupied with making arrangements and taking care of my family that I really didn't stop to breathe, let alone think about what my life would be like without Mom.

Then, leaving work on my first day back at my corporate job, I put in my Bluetooth and started to dial Mom's number. I stopped just before hitting the "Connect" button when I suddenly realized that there would be no more calls with Mom. I was overcome with grief—and something else. Suddenly it hit me: *I'm fifty-three years old, my kids are grown and my parents are gone. I'm no longer responsible for anyone but me!* Something was missing, and I needed to figure out what it was.

Until my mom passed away, I thought I knew exactly what I'd be doing the rest of my life. But now I was lost. From the time I was a young child, I had taken on the role of caregiver. I was always in the supporting role; never front and center, never asking for what I needed or wanted. (I'm not even sure I *knew* what I needed or wanted.) As the oldest of nine children, I became a caregiver at an early age. I had been in that role for so long—first with my siblings, then with my own family, and finally with my mom—that I now had no idea who I was or what I was meant to do.

It was during this time, in the weeks after losing my mom, that I sat down to look at old family slides with my sister, Tricia. We started at the beginning, flipping through image after image, laughing and remembering. At one point she joked, "You're taking care of someone in almost every picture."

That can't be true, I thought, but I looked through the slides again and she was right! There were so many pictures of me holding my siblings or mothering my own children. There was even one memorable photo of me at two-and-a-half, standing at an ironing board. It's as if I'd been living the same role for years—forever, really. I took great pride in that role, and received a lot of praise and attention for my efforts. But somewhere along the way, I lost track of a sense of purpose beyond caring for others. I had spent my whole life building other people up, and I had never learned how to do that for myself.

Without my mom to talk with, my mind was busy all the time: thinking, thinking, thinking. Maybe too much! *There has to be more than the day-to-day grind.* I began to look deep inside myself for answers. I read books, listened to experts I resonated with, and attended workshops and trainings to help me tackle the big questions: What will I leave behind when *I'm* gone? How do I want to be remembered? How can I make a real difference in the world? What legacy am I leaving my children and grandchildren?

It was these last two questions that I pondered the most and that ultimately guided me to the answer. Through the founding of Vitaerobics, a company dedicated to teaching people how to take control of their own health, my parents had made a difference and left a legacy—for us, and for the more than six-hundred-thousand people they helped along the way.

When my husband and I were given the opportunity to take over Vitaerobics, suddenly I knew that I wanted to carry on my parents' good work and create a legacy of health for generations to come. (I say "suddenly," but it was sudden in the way that a singer struggling in the shadows for years is "suddenly" discovered.) *This is my calling. I want to make a positive difference in the health and lives of others. This is who I was meant to be.* Finally, some clarity!

They say it is all about timing, and this was my time! I accepted this new challenge with excitement, but I struggled with the transition. I tried to continue operating the business as my parents would have, doing it "their way." I was afraid to make big changes, and I was even more afraid to face the reality that I would probably have to quit my safe, secure, corporate job in order to truly make a difference. I realized that to reach my true calling, I would have to be the person I knew I could be, not the person others wanted me to be.

One of my mentors suggested I work through something called a "fear" exercise to move from a place of doubt to one of true belief in myself and all I had to offer. Through this exercise, I realized, *I've been telling myself internal stories, and these stories are causing*

> *I realized that to reach my true calling, I would have to be the person I knew I could be, not the person others wanted me to be.*

me to doubt myself and my own abilities. This realization, and the understanding of how my internal stories influenced my actions, enabled me to take control and rewrite my self-defeating stories. This process helped me discover who I really was, and people could see the difference immediately. For maybe the first time in a long time, they could see the real me!

Once I began to believe in myself, doors opened and opportunities appeared—just as the Law of Attraction promises. I did my part, of course; and when I did, a clear path emerged. It was then that I became absolutely certain that my husband and I could carry on what my parents started twenty-five years ago—*and take it to the next level.*

Through my journey to find "me," I had to reach deep inside myself and learn to truly value all that I had to offer and all that I was capable of being. This was one of the hardest things I've ever done. When Mom died, I was still locked into the belief that I was here to take care of people, to play it safe and steer clear of risk. I thought my role was to support, not lead. But I wanted more out of life, and I had to learn to stop feeling guilty for wanting more. Of course, it's important to sometimes put others before oneself, but I have learned that my own needs are important too. It is a balancing act.

What I came to realize was this: We all become who we are supposed to become at the right time in our lives. Every choice I made in the past, every helping hand I offered, every person I

You will succeed because of your experiences
(all of them), not in spite of them.

---

supported, *every day I lived* led me to this point in my life. The Universe gave me the skills and experiences I needed, when I needed them.

Because of my life experiences, I became the perfect person to guide my parents' company—now *my* company—into a new future. I realized that my natural "caregiver" instincts were an asset, not a character flaw or a weakness.

All of my experiences—being the oldest of nine, having responsibilities early, caring for others—made me who I am today, and I wouldn't trade any of them. So often we look at some of the events of our lives and some of the choices we have made, and conclude that they were bad, harmful or negative. I say, throw out that thinking and use all those events and choices! Respect them. You wouldn't be the person you are today without them! You will succeed because of your experiences (all of them), not in spite of them.

It's funny how life comes together. I still miss my mom every day, but in so many ways, she is right beside me on this journey. I draw on the things she taught me every day, and I know she is so very proud of what I have become. At fifty-five, I now see that my mission is to break the cycle of obesity and health-related issues that have affected past generations and to empower women to take control of their family's health and create a healthy future for themselves and those they love.

You must believe in yourself. That begins with honoring your life experiences and trusting that everything happens as it should. Don't discard the past; let it serve you. It's all gold. Even if you're not using your voice right this minute, you are still moving forward. Maybe the time isn't right for you *right now.* Maybe, like me, you'll find the "right time" one day when you least expect it. But I promise that you *will* find it. That I know *for sure.*

Johnell Borer McCauley is passionate about making a positive difference in the health of families everywhere. A food psychology and nutrition expert, speaker and author, Johnell is the creator of Nutrition Unmasked, Vitaerobics' signature program that reveals the secrets to taking control of your health. She empowers women to create a healthy future for themselves and those they love by unraveling nutrition fact from fiction in ways that encourage immediate results and set the stage for a legacy of great health. Connect with Johnell at www.HealthyFamilyFuture.com.

Get Comfortable Being Uncomfortable

Julie Thomas

S haking, I took the cashier's check from the bank officer. I held one million dollars in my hand. Suddenly, we were in debt up to our eyeballs. This down payment on the business I was about to purchase amounted to five times the cost of my house. To make this leap, my husband and I had taken out a second mortgage and a huge chunk of capital from our family funds. I was really, really scared.

I'd worked for my company for almost sixteen years when I went on maternity leave in March of 2002 to have my second child. When I came back at the end of July, my boss's boss had been let go, and a new executive vice president of sales had been brought in from the outside. By the beginning of October, he let go of four key managers, including my direct boss, and hired all new people.

My new boss, Tim, was almost completely unresponsive. I managed a team of about ten people and a five-and-a-half-million-dollar budget, and I had good-sized responsibility in the organization; yet, my phone calls went unanswered, and my emails were ignored or answered with very clipped, curt responses. It was clear that Tim had no intention of building a relationship, and several of my peers were in the same boat. When would the next reduction in forces occur? Who would be swept away with the next wave?

When I logged on to my computer the Friday morning before Christmas and saw a very detailed email from Tim, I knew something was up. He wanted to meet in Connecticut for about an hour on the Monday between Christmas and New Year's Eve. Nobody was working that week; I lived in California and would have to fly cross-country. Ridiculous.

I picked up the phone, and for the first time, Tim actually answered my call. I backpedaled, asking, "Is there an alternative meeting time?"

Tim hemmed and hawed.

Then I said, "Tim, can I ask you a question? Is the real agenda of this meeting to tell me that my services are no longer needed?"

When would the next reduction in forces occur? Who would be swept away with the next wave?

He began to stammer. "Well, uh… yeah, we're making some changes, but I really want to have this conversation face to face. Everybody likes you; we want to treat you well."

Don't react. Don't say anything that's going to blow your severance, I thought, because I knew I wasn't being let go for a *reason.* As he stammered, I began to get really mad. *He's going to have me fly all this way and leave my family during the holidays to FIRE me? Is he kidding?*

"Why don't you just transfer me to Human Resources?" I asked. "There's no reason for us to have a meeting." HR wasn't prepared to talk to me about the severance package, because they thought I wouldn't need it until after the meeting on December 28. Merry Christmas. I hung up the phone, had a good cry and thought, *It's Friday—I'm going to go finish my Christmas shopping.*

Wow—they don't want me! On top of the anger and hurt, this was a serious blow to my ego. Even though I'd seen it coming, this was the first time I had ever lost a job—I'd never even been passed up for a promotion before. I had been at this company for sixteen years, working my way up from accounting to group vice president of professional development and sales training. My career had been on a fast-moving, positive trajectory; I'd been perceived as a top performer in every role and was well-liked and well-respected. It was deeply embarrassing to tell my staff, my peers and even my family that I'd been fired.

Thank goodness, I have a wonderful husband and am not the sole breadwinner, and the company treated me fairly in severance. Money wasn't the concern, and I wasn't worried about my ability to get a new job. But the question, "What do I do now?" brought up real fear. After all that time and effort building me to the place I had reached in the company, whatever I did, I'd be starting at ground zero. I was afraid of what that might mean. I had two little kids. Would I have to go back into a sales rep job, traveling every week with no flexibility to be at home at night with my family? That was unacceptable.

Though my husband was an executive with a Fortune 25 company and could support the family, I was a *working* mom. I worked and needed to work; work is a big part of my identity. I was raised by a single mom who didn't know, sometimes, where the next dollar would come from; so it was always very important to me to be financially independent. I bought my first home as a single woman and married at thirty-four. The option of not working and using this transition period to play more tennis didn't appeal to me at all.

As part of my separation, I was provided career counseling and job-placement services. I participated in a training workshop on entrepreneurship and found it fascinating. I began to completely expand my view of what opportunities might interest me and what my future might hold. Becoming a business owner—now that was an interesting concept. But, I still thought I would just go and be an employee somewhere else.

I had become good friends with the founder and president of a very successful sales training company, so I decided to approach him about working with him. Unbeknownst to me, he was looking for an exit strategy. This was both an excellent business opportunity and a pivotal moment—maybe my future career path did not involve being someone else's employee.

Just ninety days after I received notice at my old company, and with my husband's full support, I signed a letter of intent to purchase the sales training company. And on July 9, 2003, I handed over a check for a million dollars. Not only was my friend willing to finance the rest of the purchase, to be paid off

---

I was taking a huge risk.

---

in a balloon payment at the end of four years, he would also act as my mentor as I jumped into the heretofore unfamiliar position of general executive manager, dealing with every financial, legal and production issue I hadn't encountered before. The business decision was sound, but life taking a completely different direction than I ever anticipated was scary and uncomfortable as well as exciting and invigorating. I was taking a huge risk.

Doing something so completely new brought up a real fear of failure, and the finances were scary too. To pay off loans and interest *and* make the huge balloon payment meant working my tail off for those four years without drawing a salary. If I failed, the company would go back to the old owner, and I'd be out a million dollars—plus every installment I had paid. I had to be successful. I had to grow the business, and I had to conserve the cash to make that balloon payment in July of 2007. There was no turning back.

And, I'm so glad I didn't turn back. I've always thought of myself as adaptable and something of a risk taker, but before I was laid off it had always been within the safety net of an employment arrangement. Because I recognized early on what knowledge I had and what I lacked, I surrounded myself with people whose skills complemented my own and didn't try to do it all. "It takes a village" certainly applies to business.

In an economic downturn, one of the first things businesses cancel is training, since it is considered a discretionary expense.

But, our whole message is about how to give your sales staff the skill set to compete on value, not price. For this reason, we have actually continued to grow significantly. We made that scary balloon payment, and we've grown by about twenty percent each year since I bought the business.

Most importantly, I can't imagine my life or my lifestyle without having become the owner and operator of my business. As a working mom, I am a better role model for my children (especially my daughter). I always knew I was a good salesperson; but, I never knew I was a good *businessperson*. I never thought of myself as a public speaker or an author, but I'm now publishing my second book.

The fact is, I never knew what my true potential was, until a catalytic event—being laid off—forced me to change my thinking. It turned out that all my previous experience as a hardworking employee had actually prepared me to be an entrepreneur!

Transition is scary, so get comfortable with being uncomfortable. The push that feels fatal can be just the nudge we need to get to the next level of our personal or professional development. You can either let fear paralyze you, or you can use it as fuel to move forward. A risk or transformation

Transition is scary, so get comfortable with being uncomfortable.

will always come with some unease, and that is a good thing, because it means you're pushing yourself to reach a potential you might never have imagined for yourself before. No one gets ahead by being victimized or standing still.

If you are in transition or attracted to a new opportunity, get clear about what you're good at and what resources are available to you, whether that includes an informal network of people to advise you or a solid financial footing, and then do the work. Success is the convergence of confidence, competence and hard work. The only place that success comes before work is in the dictionary.

Julie Thomas has enjoyed a meteoric rise through the ranks of sales, sales management and corporate leadership positions on the road to her present role as President and CEO of ValueSelling Associates. She has since led the company to become an industry leader in competency- and process-based training for escalating sales performance. Julie is also a sought-after speaker, author and consultant, and a guest lecturer at Babson University and the University of Michigan. Julie has published Value Selling: Driving Sales Up One Conversation at Time *and is currently working on her second book. Connect with Julie at www.ValueSelling.com.*

Redefining Success

Rochelle Togo-Figa

"We're pretty certain it's cancer. We have to make arrangements for you to be admitted to the hospital immediately." Life stood still. I sat facing the doctor from the other side of his desk as from across a chasm, completely shocked and unable to speak. *Oh my God! I might die!* I didn't know much about breast cancer—all I knew was, you hear the C-word and it means death.

My whole life up until then, I'd never been sick. Never ever. I was only forty-three years old, and I'd always taken good care of myself. I jogged in Central Park on a regular basis. I'd even gone to a breast specialist for check-ups because my breast tissue was especially dense and fibrous, and nothing had ever been detected. I thought that cancer happened to other people, not to me.

Besides, I didn't have time for cancer. My whole life was centered on making money, getting more, and more and more. I defined success based on my income and my assets and my professional accomplishments, and I was running as fast as I could on the hamster wheel of life to get it. I was, without a doubt, one-hundred percent focused on my version of success, to the exclusion of everything else.

After a shower one day, I had examined myself and felt a lump on my left breast. I was so frightened—no denying something was there. So I'd gone to see the doctor immediately, bringing my boyfriend at the time, Rob, and another good friend for support. The doctor examined me, and then had us all sit in the waiting room. Twenty minutes later he called us in and broke the shocking news. Cancer.

The first few days after that seemed like an out-of-body experience—everything happened so quickly. I took an emergency leave of absence from my corporate job, and in a matter of days I

I didn't know much about breast cancer—all I knew was, you hear the C-word and it means death.

went through a nine-and-a-half-hour operation, during which the surgeons found that the cancer was contained in one area. I felt a huge sense of relief about that, and I was thankful to be alive.

I experienced a very real and immediate awareness of my own mortality. This was the first time in my entire life I grasped the possibility I could die. It finally hit me: *I'm not invincible. This is it.* I looked at my life, and I was so unfulfilled at my job. I'd been chasing after an idea of success that had never brought me any satisfaction.

Cancer was my wake-up call. For the first time, I looked deep into my inner self and asked, "If not now, when? What are you waiting for? What do you really want, Rochelle?" During the six months of chemo, I did a lot of self-reflection. I stopped racing. I was always so busy trying to make money, trying to be successful, that I had never slowed down. So I started meditating, listening to inspirational tapes, reading books about spiritual transformation and going to hear motivational speakers. I joined a support group. And for the first time, I listened to my inner voice. I had never quieted my mind that way before. Over time, I realized that I had to make some big changes.

I had to change the way I was thinking. I really believed that I had something to do with getting healthy, that I wasn't going to leave it up to the doctors. I did what I could; I took my healing into my own hands. I practiced changing negative thoughts into positive ones. I started journaling my step-by–step process, continually reinforcing my new mindset by realizing that in controlling my own thoughts, I could manifest anything I wanted for my life, including my healing from cancer.

Expressing my vulnerability with others and sharing my authentic self with them drew authentic, supportive people into my life. Along the way, it became clearer and clearer that if I wanted to make any changes, they were all up to me. It was time for me to stop surviving life and start thriving in it. It was time to design the life I was truly meant to live.

My plan was to move to Boston with my family during chemo and my recovery. And I'd figured that Rob, whom I'd only been dating for six months when I got the diagnosis, would probably just leave. I'd never been successful in relationships; I felt positively unlucky in love. But, Rob was so blown away by who I was and the powerful, positive way I handled the cancer that he took me

---

I'd been chasing after an idea of success that had never brought me any satisfaction.

---

completely by surprise. "I love who you are," he told me. "Up until I met you, I was only interested in myself. You have changed my life. Come live with me. We'll get through this and get you well together."

Because I had begun to let go of trying to "make it" and prove myself, the world opened up to me. And, in turn, my heart opened up to Rob. I moved in with him, and continued to take on my own recovery. We fell in love, and in going through the process of healing with him right there by my side, I realized that he was *the one*. I recovered far more quickly than the doctors expected and felt healthier and more vibrant than I ever had before I got sick. A year and a half after my surgery, Rob and I married. We have been together for almost twenty years.

I also left my corporate job, knowing its stressful environment and lack of genuine connection to my heart and soul had contributed to my getting sick. I knew I wanted to become a coach; I wanted to lead groups of people and help them move through barriers in their lives and follow their dreams. So, I took the action steps to fulfill my own dream. I went to work for a training company and trained to lead workshops. I did a personal growth workshop, which gave me the courage to move through my fears. I left the training company six-and-a-half years later and started my own business. I had always wanted to do my own thing, but I was afraid I would fail. I was afraid I wasn't smart enough. But, I realized that if I could make my life better while facing cancer, there was nothing I couldn't do.

Cancer is over. It's done. It doesn't define me, though it made me stronger, because it showed me that I could take control, change my mindset and create a life I really loved. I met my soul mate having cancer, and I started a business, a dream I always had. My illness

*It wasn't until I went through cancer
and redefined success that I was
actually able to experience it!*

allowed me to become connected to people, to who I really am and to my purpose. What I went through, and getting to the other side, *became* my purpose. I did all this on my own terms.

Before cancer, I was always trying to "make it." I never felt successful. My journey helped me learn to give that up. Success is about being connected to people, being present in the moment and making a difference for people. It's about being authentic and being connected to people from the heart. Before my illness, I was disconnected. I was trying to grab onto something that wasn't really there. Before cancer, I was trying to prove myself according to hollow, illusory concepts of making it—so I never *could* make it. And then when I got sick, the realization came that there was nowhere else to get to: *This is it.*

It wasn't until I went through cancer and redefined success that I was actually able to experience it! Success, to me, is being fulfilled, satisfied and content with my life. Success does not mean that I am the richest person monetarily; but, I'm the richest person from within, from my heart. When I know that I'm making a difference for another person and making an impact in a positive way, I know that I'm succeeding. Ultimately, success will be in feeling, at the end of it all, that my life was used for something far bigger than myself.

So many people go through life trying to be "better" or to get something, and they're never satisfied because they're living in the future, always wanting something more and looking to tomorrow. There is no future. No one knows what's in the future. It hasn't happened yet. Who you're being right now is all you have. And, if you're happy, grateful and satisfied, you'll be that way going forward.

Be grateful for where you are. Appreciate it. Success—life— is all about being present right now, rather than trying to get somewhere else. Experience living in the moment. Be present and enjoy life right now.

Rochelle Togo-Figa is a sales business coach, trainer and motivational speaker whose experience surviving breast cancer transformed her life forever. She left the corporate world to pursue her dream of helping entrepreneurs follow their dreams and goals, taking the lessons that turned her life around—together with twenty-four years' sales experience—to create a thriving coaching and training business. She is the creator of The Inner Game of Sales™, The Sales Breakthrough System™ and The Speak Like a Pro and Make Money Doing It Self-Study Program™, all teaching tools for professionals. She is also the author of the sales home-study program Sell Without the Slick.

Rochelle has coached and trained for a variety of Fortune 500 companies, including American Express, Deutsche Bank, Merrill Lynch and many others. She has been featured on national radio, in The New York Times, The Westchester Journal News *and* Business Woman Magazine, *and has been the featured speaker in many series, webinars and events. Connect with Rochelle at www.SalesBreakthroughs.com.*

From Best Supporting Actress to Leading Lady

Karen Kennedy

I was eight years old when my dad uprooted our family, moving us from history-laden Jim Crow Jackson, Mississippi to liberal Oakland, California. I was teased for my heavy accent—and for displaying the polite, respectable behaviors I thought every child learned. The culture shock was mind-boggling to me, and I felt alone and homesick.

I resented being taken from my happy home. We'd had a spacious house with a huge yard shaded by flowering trees to play in. My grandparents were there, as well as my aunts, uncles and a slew of cousins. People carried themselves with pride and dignity and treated each other with kindness and respect.

That old world seemed organized into a manageable order, while the new one felt grubby, crowded and chaotic. We lived in a small apartment and had few places to play outside. I was shocked by the rudeness of the kids in school, who would have gotten licked with the paddle back home. Here, the teachers had no discipline. And, even to my eight-year-old eyes, it was clear that most of the adults were soft.

As if the displacement wasn't bad enough, my parents started fighting and abruptly separated. They never got back together. For a while, my mom, my brother and sister and I lived in a shelter. Within a short time my parents divorced, and because it was all she could afford, my mom moved us into an apartment in a new neighborhood, one of the worst in the entire city: a ghetto littered with drug dealers and police, stray dogs and people strung out on drugs with trash everywhere. We were afraid to go outside.

My mom joined the church just outside our neighborhood. Church was a kind of oasis, a relief from the sadness of everyday life. I went to a youth program there that gave us kids something fun and safe to do on Friday nights. That's where I met Kaylin, and my whole life became bright as day.

Kaylin was four years older than I was and had skipped a grade, so he was back on Christmas break from his first year in college when I sat next to him one Friday night. I thought he was cute and sweet and smart, and as we talked about our lives and his experience in school, I was very intrigued. When he came home for summer break, we started hanging out. Often Kaylin found things for us to do just so I could get away from home; when someone cares for you, he wants better for you, and to protect you.

We became great friends, and totally fell for each other—it was puppy love, first love, epic love. Being together was never in question. We planned our whole lives together. I would go to college; then we'd get married and have four kids, two girls and two boys. We'd even named them all. I just didn't know our plans would come true so early. It's as if we spoke them into existence.

I found myself in love—and pregnant—at fifteen. I gave birth to a beautiful baby girl, Kayla, just two weeks shy of my sixteenth birthday in September. Kaylin had waited to go back to school, so he could be there for her birth. He was on a full academic scholarship at a university in Georgia, and despite pressure from our parents for Kaylin to come home right away to take care of his new family, we made the tough decision that it was ultimately better for us if he kept his scholarship and finished school. Two months after his graduation, we were married in the Reno courthouse on July 5, 1997. I was sixteen and pregnant with our second daughter, Akayli.

It was a great love story—we were proud of it, and we were really happy for a long time. But, there was a lot of pressure on both of us.

Just out of school, Kaylin had the huge responsibility of providing for four people. He landed a great job making great money, but he sometimes regretted that he couldn't enjoy the fruit of all his hard work, seeing his friends drive nice cars, go on vacations and just hang out doing young-people stuff. I was in the same boat, sometimes envying my friends' freedoms and young-people issues. I didn't have much in common with eleventh-graders anymore. I was a wife and mother of two, finishing high school in independent studies so I could be home with my girls and driving to school to turn in my homework every week. It was a lot. Sometimes Kaylin and I resented each other for it.

Often, when I tried hard to work on the marriage, Kaylin was on autopilot. Then later, when he was ready to try, I was shut down. Gradually, we both became unhappy. He would go to work and be gone ten or twelve hours. When he came home, the house was always perfect, the kids (now three girls, with Kaytlin) beautiful and happy, his dinner cooked. I waited to eat with him, no matter the hour. Now, he came in and disappeared into our office to

I found myself in love—and
pregnant—at fifteen.

drown himself in video games. He withdrew from our relationship completely; it hurt me terribly. My family was my whole world, and his rejection made me feel worthless. Much later, when we became good friends again, I told him, "We just kept missing each other."

It wasn't long before my spirit was completely shattered. *What is wrong with me? Why am I not enough?* I tried to be a perfect wife and mother. My girls never went to daycare. I taught them everything. We went to play groups, took mommy and baby swim classes together, fed ducks at the pond, went to the zoo. I woke up with Kaylin in the morning and cooked him breakfast before he went to work, drove to have lunch with him sometimes during the week, tried and tried to get him to see me and love me again. Everything I did was for my family.

I had the dream so many women wanted to fulfill: I was married, a stay-at-home mom of beautiful children in a brand-new house my husband had bought me, with two respectable vehicles in the driveway. If I brought up my troubles, I heard, "What could you possibly have to complain about? How could *you* be unhappy?"

During a conversation with one of my best friends, she told me what I already knew: "If you don't leave now, you may wind up hurting him or yourself." The latter had already begun to happen.

I knew I had to leave.

I was severely depressed. I had nightmares and couldn't sleep. I either overate or ate nothing at all, and my weight was up and down like a yo-yo. Sometimes I couldn't stop crying. I would slip into our big walk-in closet that didn't share a wall with any other room in the house, shut the door and put my arms around myself, holding myself as tightly as I could, and just rock and cry myself to sleep. Sometimes I cried until I popped blood vessels in my eyelids. When I started cutting myself, I knew something had to give.

I knew I had to be strong and find a way for my daughters—and for myself—even if I didn't know who I was or where I was going. I did, however, know where I was NOT going: back to the ghettos I grew up in when my parents divorced. I wasn't going to let my daughters experience the emptiness I felt when my family disbanded. So, I made a very strategic exit, one that made our separation gradual and amicable. I didn't want to leave hating him. I didn't want to come into the world for the first time as a bitter woman. "Plan your work and work your plan." I'd heard that somewhere—and I had my work cut out for me. But, I knew I had to leave. If I hadn't, I might not be here telling this story now.

The day I filed for divorce from my husband, I couldn't help feeling defeated. *This cold, cruel life has won.* Then about a month later, Mark, my close friend, was killed in a car accident. That deepest heartache made me realize that life was too short and precious to waste being angry and unhappy. "Whatever it looks like for you," I told Kaylin with tears in my eyes, "I want you to be happy." We both wanted the right thing for our family—growing up together in our marriage had simply taken its toll on us.

On my own for the first time in my life, I had to learn to trust and believe in myself. I didn't have Kaylin taking care of me or Mark's encouragement. I had to be all that and more for myself, by myself. Kaylin remained a great dad and provider to our daughters. But, as the head of household, I was in a new role. There was no room for the crippling story that I wasn't enough, because I *had* to be enough. I was all I had, and my daughters depended on me.

When I found myself as unhappy with my career as I was in my marriage, I reached again to that core inner strength I'd found to move on from my marriage. I decided I wouldn't work for anyone else again. Being from the South and knowing about finishing schools, I recognized there weren't many in the Bay Area. I'd seen how valuable proper etiquette was in business practice, especially

Finally, I'm proud of me.

when I worked for a Fortune 500 investment company in Silicon Valley. I'd started crafting an outline for my own program in my spare time while working and decided to launch a new career as an entrepreneur. It was fitting to create work tailored to who I was and what I was great at. That turned out to be Southern manners and hospitality and a natural eye for decorating and fashion. I found the courage to believe in myself. I give back by helping other people to blossom, teaching adults how proper etiquette can transform their personal and professional lives.

For a long time, I felt deep shame that I was a teenage mother, that my marriage failed and that I didn't feel good enough. The story of my life remained a dark secret. But, with time, I realized my experiences were not happening *to* me, they were happening *for* me. I learned that growing up in the ghetto and being a teen parent did not have to define who I am. My spouse did not define who I am. I do.

I tell my daughters—three brilliant, beautiful, happy girls I am so proud of every single day—that they get to choose exactly what kind of people they want to be. "You have a special seven-year-old power," I told Kaytlin, my youngest. "You can choose what kind of daughter, sister and kid you want to be." I wish someone had told me that when I was fifteen, but now I'm the one who can say it to myself. *You have to live for yourself first. Accept this new role in your life—you're the leading lady now, not the supporting actress. You can be whatever you choose to be.* Finally, I'm proud of me.

As spring brings a new life to a flower, each day brings a new beginning for us all. We have to trust and believe in ourselves. We have to be okay with the fact that things may not be great now, but know there is power within us to turn them around. Find successes you've had in other places in your life and apply those same strategies to present-day problems. Are you an extra in the movie of your life, or are you ready to blossom out of old beliefs about yourself and claim your starring role?

Karen Kennedy founded Lady Blossoms Social Etiquette Program & Services in 2011. As a social etiquette coach and speaker, she imparts the tools and resources for raising your social interactions to a new high standard to create opportunity for personal and professional success. Services also include wardrobe consulting, personal shopping and interior decorating. Her popular CD, Lady Blossoms' Top 10 Rules of Etiquette, *is available in both English and Spanish on her website. She is also the co-author of* Socially Smart and Savvy, *a contemporary guide to presenting your best self in every way, every time. She holds degrees in social and behavioral science and in liberal arts, and has studied communications. "Lady K" lives in the San Francisco Bay Area and has three wonderful daughters who inspire her every day. Connect with her at www.LadyBlossoms.net.*

Finding Joy

Michelle Robin, DC

God, if this is really all there is to life, making money and pretending to be somebody day in and day out, then please check me out. I've done my assignment. I want to leave.

Driving home from my thriving chiropractic practice one day in August 1997, I found myself praying for a way out of my life.

I always thought I was getting *someplace*—that once I became a doctor, I'd be somebody. Then I thought that once I had my own house, I'd be somebody. The latest thought had been, *If I build my own practice....*

It hadn't worked. After spending five years building it, I had the practice of my dreams, and I still felt like nobody. In fact, I felt totally empty and dead inside. I knew I was successful. I was valued and liked and even loved, but I didn't feel truly connected to anyone.

In my world, the light was all coming from the outside; on the inside I was very dark. This feeling of emptiness was not new, but it had finally become intolerable. I wasn't aware of it at the time, but I was carrying around significant, unresolved pain. Like many people, I'd had a challenging upbringing. Mine was in an alcoholic household where I experienced sexual abuse, abandonment and other forms of chaos. I could not remember a time when I felt good enough.

When I again found myself praying to die but feeling too scared to take action, I gripped the steering wheel and thought, *I've got to do something different from what I'm doing now.* I got home from work and called my minister. "Mary, I don't know what to do anymore." I told her about all the dark thoughts I'd been having.

To my surprise, she said, "Michelle, I've been waiting for your call. And, I recommend you do a little exploration and address the lack of joy in your life. What do you think is holding you back from joy?"

I began a journey to find an answer to that question. So many people are driving to get someplace or to overcome some huge obstacle, not realizing that they are somebody, and they have been

---

In my world, the light was all coming from the outside; on the inside I was very dark.

---

somebody all along the way. Nothing gained on the outside is ever going to fix the inside.

Before I reached my moment of crisis in 1997, I vividly remembered hearing a woman speak about leaving her "successful" life behind to go live in a tiny cabin in Colorado and write. The reaction from the audience was mostly puzzlement: "Why would she do a thing like that?" Even then I remember thinking, *Maybe she's the one who's right, and we're the ones who have it all backwards. What looks like a simple life on the outside might look happier on the inside too.*

When I began my journey, I really had to dig around inside and ask, *What is driving me? What is driving my visions, my dreams?* It was this fear that I would never be good enough. My long-standing belief was that if I just did enough for somebody, they would love me. And, I'd been striving so hard to "be somebody" on the outside that I'd totally disconnected from who I was on the inside and what I really felt. I realized that I didn't really want to commit suicide; I just could no longer live without being present in my own life.

So, I started to deal with the anger I felt toward my mother and looked at the behavioral patterns I'd developed as a people pleaser. And, I began questioning some of the mantras I'd been reciting to myself for years without even realizing what I was telling myself: *You think you have it bad, look at the kids in Africa. Who do you think you are? You could have been _____. You should have done _____.* I knew I was on the path to healing when I no longer blamed my mother for any of my journey, but saw her compassionately, as another person who had suffered. Then, I was able to let go and begin to actually love myself.

Throughout my journey, I discovered who I was and learned to fall in love with the essence of me: the Michelle here right now, present in this moment. I found my joy and an internal knowing that I am somebody; I am enough, right now, in the present moment.

Success on the inside is at least as important as success on the outside. How many people do you know who seem to have so much going for them—they look great on stage—but when you

---

Success on the inside is at least as important as success on the outside.

---

look underneath the attractive surface, you find out their marriage is a shambles, their kids don't like them and they're depressed and in poor health? I see this outward success plus inward despair all the time in my practice. Fifteen years ago, my message would have been very different; it was most important to me to succeed in spite of the legacy of my childhood. Now, I know that I would rather have nothing and be alive inside than have everything on the outside and feel dead on the inside.

I believe that true success is learning how to triumph over that monkey mind we all suffer from—what I call "The Committee," the collection of voices that chimes "shoulda, woulda, coulda" in your mind all day and tries to make you live someone else's dreams rather than your own. I still battle it all the time. But, it is really a triumph to show up every day and listen for the real you underneath the chatter, no matter what is happening in your life and no matter what you are trying to achieve or overcome. Being present with yourself, you naturally start to align who you are and want to be with the actions you are taking to create the life you want. You align your *being* with your *doing*.

Once you let go of the monkey mind, become present in your life and start to fall in love with the essence of who you are, it's amazing how much easier it is to take care of yourself. All addiction stems from a lack of self-love. Many health problems arise from not loving ourselves enough to make ourselves a priority. We say we care about wellness (*being*), and yet we don't take the actions that create that wellness (*doing*). If life is based on what I do rather than who I am, that's a problem. And, that's the problem in America. It's a big reason we're so unhealthy as a population.

When I work with a patient, I always try first to get her to listen to and care enough about herself that she will take the time to drink water. She will take the time to sleep at night. Women, especially, are notorious for overcommitting. We say "yes" to that networking group, and "yes" to that dinner date and "yes" to over-scheduling our children, all of which, in turn, truly has an impact on our health. We don't have time to eat right; we don't have time to exercise; and we don't have time to spend on our relationships. We don't say "yes" to ourselves. We don't give ourselves the same love and caring we so readily give others.

I actually create white space in my calendar. I have exercise on my calendar every day. I have yoga twice a week. I have time with my friends. And, I may not have anything scheduled in a spot, but I block it out so that when I look at my calendar, I remember to make time for me. Somebody'll say, "Can you go out to breakfast?"

If I look at my calendar, and it has "yoga," I have to make that decision: Am I going to give up my workout time—or my time to be present with myself alone—to see somebody else? Scheduling time with yourself is so important. Make a date with yourself on the calendar consistently. You can always choose to change plans, but I find that if I don't at least put me on the calendar, I'll overbook myself. I'm not quite savvy enough yet to put myself first and work after, but I would say I'm heading in the right direction. Self-love and self-care are always a journey.

Why do we feel guilty about taking time for ourselves? It actually should be liberating to say "no" when "no" is the true answer coming from our heart. A big difference in my life recently is when somebody asks me to do something, I will do the opposite of what I once did as a people pleaser and say "no" first instead of "yes." Typically, we say "yes" first, and then think (or complain to someone else), "Oh no! I really don't want to. Now how do I get out of it?"

Say "no" first! When I'm asked to do something that doesn't resonate with me, I'll say, "It doesn't quite feel like it's mine to do— I'll let you know if that changes." I'm not offering an excuse; I'm just being present to my own truth in that moment. Not too long

---

Say "no" first!

---

ago, I was asked to be on a heart association board. I thought about it for a while: *Gosh, I get to work with all the heads of the hospitals in the city. What a great position to be in!* But, I also dreaded the idea and could not deny that something inside me said, *No! You're not passionate about it.* So I said, "You know what? Thank you, but this is not really congruent with what I believe." I believe in well-being. There are heart associations and diabetes associations and cancer associations—where is the well-being association? That's where I'm signing up.

Why is it that we have to get sick before we start living? Why do we prioritize and feed our fire into what simply stresses us out? We need to save our energy so that we can be fully present for important experiences, such as sitting with a friend whose spouse has just died or reconnecting with childhood interests and desires. If we take care of ourselves, we have a much greater capacity to show up for those experiences. Knocking ourselves out to live other people's dreams just doesn't look as urgent when we love and care for ourselves.

I still have difficult moments occasionally. But, I also feel such a deep sense of peace and gratitude for my life now. I can forgive and stay out of a place of judgment both with myself and others, including my mother, with whom I now have a healthy relationship. I know how I want to live and contribute to the world. I know how to live from my heart and not from fear.

Recently, I was home alone on a Friday night with the dogs while my partner was traveling. I felt so happy just to have that time to be with myself, I was pleased and surprised. I thought back to the old days, when I was constantly running and never alone. I always had to hide in a large group. *You've come a long way, Michelle. You could be out with any number of people, and here you are choosing to just spend time with yourself.* It's been quite a journey: I found my joy, and I'm okay hanging with me; I'm enough.

Michelle Robin, DC, has been involved in wellness for nearly three decades. She founded Your Wellness Connection, one of the nation's most successful integrative healing centers. She also assists businesses, non-profits and faith-based communities in developing wellness programs. She actively seeks to share her wellness message through local and national speaking engagements as well as collaborative efforts with other wellness practitioners and affiliates. She wrote the acclaimed Wellness on a Shoestring: Seven Habits for a Healthy Life. *Her latest book,* The E Factor: Engage, Energize, Enrich – Three Steps to Vibrant Health, *will be released later this year. Dr. Robin is very active in the community and has received many awards; The Masters Circle recognized her as 2007 Chiropractor of the Year, and she was honored with the Speaking of Women's Health "Glow" Award (2010), and the eWomenNetwork Femtor "Made it to a Million" Award (2011). Connect with Dr. Robin at www.DrMichelleRobin.com and learn more about wellness at www.YourWellnessConnection.com.*

The Surprise Vision

Katherine Fossler

Looking back, I realize that what sprang forth as a passionate, inexplicable, incredibly strong vision was actually unearthed from somewhere deep inside of me—a glimmer of what was to be. Intuitively, I had sensed its stirring for a while.

It started when I took part in a women's weekend retreat. We were asked to close our eyes, meditate on our ideal life and then journal about it. I wrote about having a place where women could come and be themselves, where they could be accepted at face value and become empowered. After that, we were asked to create vision boards about our ideal life. As I paged through magazines, I found myself selecting images of women laughing, talking and working out. I thought, "How interesting! This doesn't jibe with what I'm doing at the church AT ALL."

That was in February of 2008, and the following October I was let go from the large church where I served as Parish Administrator. I knew it was coming—something was off. I felt it—like something heavy in the air, a thick, low cloud. The church was having serious financial issues, and many people were being laid off. I was not included in the usual council meetings I had attended monthly, nor asked for my input into the budget for the fast-approaching New Year. Still, when I said good-bye to my husband Terry on the morning of my termination, I didn't expect to be home by noon.

My termination was handled by two newly elected council volunteers, who nervously read a prepared statement. It was basically good-bye and good luck—and, by the way, we don't participate in unemployment.

"That's cool," I said. "May I clean out my office now?" I walked out and saw the pastor talking to some of the people who directly reported to me. I heard later that they were told not to have contact with me—or any of the other people who were let go—or they would suffer consequences.

There are a lot of fear and complicated politics in the culture of any church, so I wasn't surprised when only one person called later to see if I was okay.

I collected my things, pausing for a moment to text my daughter and husband: "got fired not kidding." Then I went home and pondered what to do next. I was still pondering that evening when one of my daughters phoned and asked if I would go to a new type of fitness class with her on Sunday—"to cheer you up," she said. For

The church was having serious financial issues, and many people were being laid off.

a couple of days, I laid low and regrouped, trying not to be swept away by stress. The first time I ventured out, I joined my daughter for the class. The new type of fitness was pole dancing—and not only was I instantly good at it; I fell in love with it immediately. I was amazed at how *at home* I felt. The first ten minutes of class ignited an unrelenting, unreasonable, unshakeable obsession within me. "I HAVE to bring this to other women!"

At the time, the studio we visited for that first class was the only place in Minneapolis offering pole dancing, and the gals teaching were real exotic dancers who worked in the clubs at night. Their boyfriends hung out in the parking lot with the rims spinning on their Escalades, waiting to whisk their ladies away to their evening jobs. Right away, I pictured what I would do if I were teaching the class. I would create a friendly, welcoming, safe environment where women could be themselves, giggle, laugh, get fit, have fun and make friends. I would clean it up and make it classier. A vision of my own studio began to emerge.

I became totally, totally obsessed. I was going to learn those moves! I was going to teach other women! I was going to get certified as an instructor, so I could teach with skill, confidence

A vision of my own studio began to emerge.

and safe methods! The driving force was to create a classy place where every woman who walked through the door was totally supported, loved and accepted at face value, no matter where she came from or what she looked like.

When I sat down with Terry and explained my plans, he gave me a funny look and asked, "This isn't just some crazy idea because of what happened with the church, is it?"

I explained how I was so consumed by this new vision that I couldn't eat, sleep or think of anything else, and I needed to see where it took me.

He looked me in the eye and said, "I'm there." (That's why I love that man!)

The next day he installed a pole in the basement. I bought some DVDs and had them express mailed, and after I put my son on the school bus in the morning I taught myself to dance. I had six weeks to train before my certification class in Las Vegas. The program was non-refundable and pretty darn expensive—talk about motivation. When I was able to teach myself to dance, pass the certification AND get better every day, it was huge. It was the cornerstone of the confidence I knew I needed to be able to pull this off.

I hired Terry, who worked as a contractor, to build the studio. We guessed at everything—how far apart to space the poles, what type of floor would be best, where to put mirrors. After the space had been rented and construction began, I had a moment of real doubt. I'd depleted my retirement fund to do all this, and charged my certification program on our already maxed-out credit card. Sitting at the kitchen table alone, I thought—for the very first time ever—*What if this doesn't work?* I instantly felt sweaty, nauseous and shaky. But then almost immediately the calm, determined feeling I'd had since the very beginning returned, and a soft, steady voice within me said, *Katherine, why would the universe set you up to fail?* I knew it would not.

I was fired on October 23, 2008, and had my open house on Valentine's Day, 2009. Wow, had I been busy! I had taught myself to dance, become a certified instructor, created classes, schedules, pricing, marketing, a logo, tagline and website. I had built a studio. I had prepared everything, spread the word and mailed out invites. I knew in my heart that the response to the open house would be a reflection of the studio's fate.

When the parking lot started to fill up and people flooded into the studio to enjoy refreshments, register for classes and even buy my tank tops, I was humbled and overjoyed! Over 350 people came to Lady Katherine that day, and I did demonstrations of pole fitness to standing-room-only crowds. I knew then that my vision was born from the desire of all those who came and all those who would come—that was its source and its purpose.

I started with weekly fitness classes of pole dance, abs and booty and exotic dance for fitness. With my classes, I made pole dancing into something with a fun, sassy and broad appeal to ordinary women like me who were stay-at-home moms, working moms, executives. They responded with such incredible enthusiasm that I was provided with continual love, appreciation and confirmation: *I have done the right thing.*

The best part is watching women become themselves, free to experience their full feminine essence. Every week I see a woman's life transformed. Last week, it was Kate, a married, working mom of two. One of her daughters has special needs, and Kate stopped me after class to tearfully share with me how Lady Katherine has awoken something inside of her she thought had died permanently. She shared how being a mom of a special-needs child required a lot, and she had no longer felt attractive or even thought of being attractive; but, her experience at my studio connected her with the place inside where she was still a vital, vibrant woman and always will be. She just forgot it was there. Now, she can walk into a room and own it.

I have heard many stories of women who have been abused finding healing and freedom through this body movement; women who found courage to leave bad relationships, unfulfilling jobs and limiting situations. It's really a makeover from the inside out. That connection with her body as a woman and that healing power reengages a woman's sense of her authentic self, so she can harness her true power. I've had so many students tell me, "I feel strong." I know they mean emotionally strong as well as physically strong.

I am in the confidence business. That's my service. When you learn to move like this, you learn to accept people for who they are, and you learn to accept yourself where you are. Confidence

---

*The best part is watching women
become themselves, free to experience
their full feminine essence.*

---

in their true selves is something so many women are searching for, often without even knowing it. At fifty-two, it's amazing to be so integrated into my physical body that I feel I can do anything. I have the freedom to take risks, to represent *myself* and not a religious institution. I'm not the church lady anymore.

I am so grateful I was fired, because it gave me the freedom, opportunity and space to take on new experiences and to discover and begin to fulfill my life's purpose, versus remaining complacent and "safe." I am grateful for the transformation, joy and purpose that other women are finding because I did. I have become so much more intuition-driven. Many days, I get up and do what my spontaneous self directs me to do—nothing more and nothing less. I hope one day to live one-hundred percent in this place of true connection and inspiration.

To this day, three-and-a-half years later, it still amazes me how I got to where I am, with two studios and hundreds of parties and workshops and thousands of classes going every year. It's a really odd-sounding transition. I went into church administration because I wanted to love, help and support people. Unfortunately, that was difficult to do most days at the church. Now, I can do it every day, but instead of wearing a business suit, I am wearing yoga pants and stripper shoes to do it!

Set your course going forward based on where you are. Don't put your blinders on. Listen to what you are sensing and look carefully at it. If a vision feels right, go for it with all your heart, passion and joy. It will not set you up to fail; it will not lead you astray; it will not let you down—so do not give doubt a moment of your time.

Set aside some time to articulate your vision from your heart onto paper. Before you do, calm yourself and call in every sense—not just your five senses, but your intuitive sense, too, that higher knowing and deeper sense of self.

Intuition will show you more than you ever expected to see!

Katherine Fossler, aka Lady Katherine, empowers women nationwide to embrace their inner beauty and ignite their feminine essence for true personal transformation. She brings credibility and accessibility to her beloved sport of pole dance with a premier Instructor Certification Program and will be franchising her Lady Katherine Women's Fitness Studios within the United States. To further help women pursue passionate, purposeful lives, she has become a speaker and certified dream coach. Connect with Katherine at www.Lady-Katherine.net.

In the Face of Conflict, Be More

Alexis Neely, Esq.

Think back to the last time you were in the midst of a conflict or a facing challenge. Was your natural response to be more or less? Did you feel great about who you were and how you showed up (or are showing up now) in reaction to the conflict? Or did you shrink and behave in ways you are not proud of today?

How do you feel in your body when you think about this conflict or challenge? Do you feel light, relaxed and free? Or constricted, heavy and as if you know you could have handled things differently?

The normal response to conflict and challenge in our culture is to be less, hold back, fight for what's rightly ours, get lawyers if we think we have been wronged, go to court and win at any cost.

This is why there are wars throughout the planet, why we believe there are not enough resources and why so many people are living with anxiety and depression. But, it does not have to be this way.

In fact, each conflict and challenge could be the direct pathway to everything you have ever wanted.

More joy, happiness, freedom and abundance are yours, now. All you need to do is shift the way you have handled conflict and challenge. Really.

My life completely shifted once I discovered what most people simply have no idea about—but you will after reading this chapter.

I cannot wait to hear how life shifts for you when you read my story, do the exercises and apply what you learn.

I've enjoyed some pretty spectacular "successes" in my life. I graduated at the top of my class from Georgetown University Law Center and began my legal career at the best law firm in the United States. Just three years after I graduated, I opened my own law firm as a solo practitioner. I've written a bestseller, made frequent TV appearances and grown multiple million-dollar companies. But, none of that is what really matters.

What I think you would find far more interesting and relevant to your life are the equally spectacular "failures"—the crises, the challenges and the conflicts that have really made me who I am.

There has been so much difficulty that at times I thought for sure I didn't really deserve the success I had achieved. I must be a bad person who deserves to be punished instead. Over and over again, I experienced situations that validated that belief. More

---

Every crisis, challenge or conflict
is your greatest opportunity to be
more of who you really are.

---

and more, I became sure that the hardships in my life were the consequences of my own lack and not-good-enoughness. Until I woke up and realized that I was not being punished at all, that I was being gifted. My job was only to see the gift and respond from a place of awareness and truth. (Easier said than done in the face of deep conditioning, so only read on if you want to try.)

Every crisis, challenge or conflict is your greatest opportunity to be more of who you really are. When you begin to recognize this truth and take action from this place, everything shifts. Conflicts become something to look forward to, because they are your chance to be more (and thereby invite more). The part that can be difficult is that "being more" in the face of conflict will almost always look a whole lot like giving up the one thing you least want to let go of—be it a belief, a thing, a person or an idea.

To make this shift in your own experience, try this:

Step 1. Contemplate the three most important qualities you want to experience in your life no matter what else is going on around you, and write them down. For me, they are generosity, love and freedom.

Step 2. Write down one situation in which you do not feel these qualities (the ones you wrote down) showing up in your life.

Step 3. Ask yourself the hard questions: How can I be more (insert your three qualities) in this situation? What can I let go of now that will allow me to be more of these qualities?

Step 4. Make a list of what you can let go of and ways you can show up differently when you are being these three qualities (even when you most do not want to) in response to a specific experience in your life. How can you *be* more?

This process of being more in the face of conflict (especially when I do not want to be), has transformed my life, and it will do the same for yours.

In 2005, while I was in the midst of a divorce and angrily fighting with my ex, most friends urged me to dig in, keep what was mine and go to battle. Yet, one close friend said something different. She repeatedly told me, "He can't hurt you."

I couldn't understand that, because it sure *seemed* as though he was hurting me when he yelled or called me names in front of my children. But, one day something shifted, and I got it, clear as a sunny day in Colorado: *This is my choice. I do not have to shrink and become small and reactive. I can be more.*

I began to see this painful time of conflict as a gift—a calling from evolution: *Be more now.*

So what did more *mean?* That was the first thing I had to understand.

I began to connect to the truth of who I really am, separate from how or what anybody else is being or doing in the world: *Generous. Loving. Free. I can be that no matter what else is happening around me. No matter what he is doing. I can be more.*

I decided to stop fighting with my ex. I asked myself what a generous, loving and free person would do, and I agreed to buy him out of the law practice I had started two years earlier and give him several thousand dollars per month in alimony and child support, so he could feel comfortable and safe.

> *Grace is the experience of knowing*
> *and behaving as if everything that*
> *goes "wrong" is a divine gift.*

That choice became the driver for me to get really serious about my business. Within one year, I had incorporated my former sole proprietorship and transformed it into a real business that went on to bring in more than a million dollars a year in revenue.

Looking back now, I can see my business's financial success was a direct reward for making the choice to be more in the face of conflict, even when every fiber of my being wanted me to keep resisting, keep fighting, be right and keep what was mine, damn it!

Had I resisted my ex then, I might *still* be locked in conflict seven years later. (Do you know any family members so dug into fights that they are dealing with the fallout years and years later?) Instead, we now co-parent our children, live in harmony on our farm and *mostly* get along great. It's not all peaches and cream, rainbows and lollipops, trust me. We still have conflict, challenge and crisis; but, now I see these difficulties for what they are—gifts, opportunities, *grace*. Grace is the experience of knowing and behaving as if everything that goes "wrong" is a divine gift.

Today, in fact, you might look at my life from the outside and think it's at a low point. I have more apparent challenges than I have ever had before. I am facing a lawsuit from a former client of my law firm; considering bankruptcy to deal with half a million dollars in debt taken on while building my earlier businesses; and living in a smaller home than I have lived in for years (we went from oceanfront in Hermosa, California to 5,300 square feet on a lake in Colorado, and now to a small three-bedroom farmhouse that reminds me of the first house I bought more than ten years ago).

Ironically, though, *my life is better than it's ever* been. I am living in alignment with the qualities I want to express. I am generous, loving and free.

I am striving far less than I ever have before, and yet more of what I really want is coming to me than ever before: meaningful friendships with other women; partnership (in life and business) with my lover; tight connection with my children; co-parenting relationship with my kids' dad; plenty of clients; opportunities to

---

Choose to be more of who you really are,
especially when you want to be less.

---

make an impact broadly and deeply; and, yes, plenty of money. In fact, I think (worry) about money far less now than I did the year I had two million in revenue. (Yep, it's really true. More money is not the answer—more *you* is where it's at, my friend.)

Right now, I invite you to more. In this very moment, whatever your circumstances are, *be more*. Making millions or living on loans; harmonious life full of ease and light or a life of trauma, disappointment and pain—*be more*.

Ask yourself who and how you want to be, and write it all down. Let go of anything (*ANYTHING*) not in alignment with you being those qualities. Just let it go.

Be prepared with the support you need so that the next conflict, challenge or crisis you face can be your greatest opportunity to be more of who you really are. Watch the magic happen.

You truly are the master of your own destiny, because YOU make the choice. Choose to be more of who you really are, especially when you want to be less.

221

Remind yourself:

This challenge is a gift.
Knowing it is grace.
Grace brings ease.
Trust.
There are no accidents.
God is benevolent,
and you are infinitely supported.

Be more of who you really are. Yes, now. I love you.

Alexis Neely, Esq., called the Good Lawyer and a business priestess by those who know her, has built two million-dollar businesses, published the best-selling book on legal planning for parents and appeared on many of the top television shows as a legal expert, all while raising two kids and waking up to a life of true freedom. Today, Alexis is making art out of supporting you to make empowered and informed legal, insurance, financial and tax (LIFT) decisions for your life and business and helping lawyers build profitable businesses that provide an extraordinary level of service, impact and fulfillment. Request a preview copy of her next book, You Are Not Your Credit Score: 9 Myths, Lies and Legends About the Credit System That Is Keeping You From Living Your Dream Life Right Now *at her website: www.EyesWideOpenLife.com.*

Where God Places You, You Will Not Fail

Shelley Oglan

"I'm ready to come clean with you, Shelley. If I send you a plane ticket, will you come?"

It's Darrin—out of the blue, three years later. I take a deep breath: *So, he's finally ready to be authentic. This is huge.*

When my husband Darrin and I parted, I had already forgiven him for everything. But, my journey to that forgiveness was slow and agonizingly hard-won. Ultimately, it was a journey of self-love and self-discovery. It was for me. I forgave him unconditionally not for him but *for myself*, so I could finally let go of my pain and find peace.

Darrin was always my soul mate, the man who loved me instantly and unconditionally, the man who went through physical beatings for me, the man who had his life threatened for dating me, the man who would not give up on me, the man who took my two children as his own, the man who saved my life, the man who stuck with me through counseling week after week for years while I painfully struggled to put my life in functional order, the man who became my husband and my best friend.

People often perceived us as an odd couple, but the truth is that, when we met, I was so ugly on the inside and he was so beautiful. His unconditional love, support and trust helped enable me to tear down, brick by brick, the wall that I had built over the years to shelter all the pain of my past. As time passed, I blossomed inside because of him. He made me who I am.

After the birth of our son, I wanted to fulfill one more goal, my education. I devised a mythical enterprise for a term paper while completing my human resources certification. My imaginary automotive parts supplier company came to fruition and experienced unprecedented growth, becoming a multi-million-dollar company within the first four years.

We did it! Or, so I thought. Starting from nothing, we built a good life, a well-respected family and a very successful business.

*I was so ugly on the inside and
he was so beautiful.*

We had it all—we were living the dream! I was so busy working and building the business for years, and I wanted to fully embrace motherhood and become a stay-at-home mom. And so it was.

It wasn't the rape I suffered at age four; it wasn't my dysfunctional, alcoholic and chaotic upbringing; the nine different schools I attended, only officially completing grade seven; the poverty, the housing projects, the drugs; getting pregnant the first time I had sex at age fifteen, the marriage a week after I turned sixteen, the abusive relationship that followed, or the divorce after six years while I was pregnant with my second child that knocked me down. No, I am a fighter and damn good at it!

The most excruciating blow—and the fight of my life—actually came two years after I retired from the business to be a full-time mom and sixteen years into the marriage. I was totally shocked to discover that my husband, my soul mate and my business partner had betrayed me on the deepest level. His infidelity with a neighbor and friend was only the first thing to be exposed. Weeks, months and even years went by before I finally knew the full depth of his deceit.

The price for his infidelities, partying, business deals and betrayals cost us everything we ever worked for. We had to file for bankruptcy both personally and professionally. The affairs, the loss of our business, the potential loss of our marriage, the public disgrace, the loss of our entire future and the cost to our family knocked me down pretty hard. It seemed like one blow after another, and they just kept coming.

My whole world was rocked! I was stripped of everything, as by a thief in the night. My soul died, and this time I didn't think I could get back up, let alone fight. Everything I ever worked for was gone; everything I ever stood for was gone; everything I ever believed in was gone. I felt raped and betrayed all over again. And, believe me, this emotional rape was far more invasive than the physical rape I endured at four years old.

I was one of the lucky few to make it out of the ghetto coming from the life I had—and now you want to knock me down with all this? Why? Couldn't you have hit me with one blow at a time? No—you have to give it to me all at once! How much can one person bear?

Overwhelming feelings of anger, bitterness, resentment, fear, embarrassment, shame, sadness and confusion flooded my mind

---

I finally knew the full depth of his deceit.

---

along with all the *whys*. Raped, stripped to nothing—betrayed, this time, by the very man who helped me save my life—the ugliness inside that I had worked so hard to transform came right back with a vengeance, directed straight at my husband, and my wall this time was made of steel.

And, one more blow—more like a technical knockout—to top it all off: We were moving to Mexico because of my husband's new employment.

The fallout of Darrin's choices had embarked us on a roller-coaster ride into our future, starting with our move. I was already devastated by the reality of having lost EVERYTHING that meant anything to me—my husband, my family, our home, our business, our friends, our life. Now, I would be taken from the only support I had, my blessed friends. I would be separated from my two older children; we would be living in three different countries. What was there to look forward to?

Mexico was a living hell. Moving there knowing no one, I was separated from my support system, learning a new culture and an unfamiliar language while trying to keep the family together and pretending everything was okay for the sake of our young son. But, what always mattered most to me was having the strength and perseverance to break the generational chains of addiction, poverty and dysfunction that ran in both sides of my family, so I could spare my children and the generations to follow. I was determined to give my son a better life, and I remained passionate about my purpose through the long and vicious fight for my life.

My heart was in such conflict! I had been so deeply wounded—I was hurt; the unresolved hurt turned to anger; the unresolved anger turned to resentment; and the resentment made me a bitter person. This whole experience ripped my heart in two. One half of my heart was filled with anger and bitterness, and the other half was filled with love and forgiveness. If I wanted my heart whole again and to really put this behind me and move forward, I would have to let go of anger and bitterness and let love and forgiveness win. "When you harbor bitterness, happiness will dock elsewhere."

The turning point came when a quote from Emerson Eggerichs hit me like a ton of bricks: "The other person doesn't cause you to be who you are, they only reveal who you're being."

I realized I needed to stop blaming my husband, and I needed his forgiveness, too! I had been behaving like that "ugly" old self again, armored in the steel wall he could not penetrate, blaming him for everything. My words cut like a knife. We both had our faults in the marriage. I wasn't any better. As always, with him, it was "no questions asked." His forgiveness was as unconditional as his love had always been.

At last, I experienced the beauty of true forgiveness for myself and for others. I chose to truly forgive Darrin unconditionally, even though I knew he still wasn't being truthful. I forgave him, not for him but for me, so I could have back my heart that I'd worked so hard on for so many years. I asked for his forgiveness, too. Our absolute forgiveness for each other enabled me to relate to him with restored love, and ironically, I also truly forgave my parents through the process. I realized, for the first time in my life, that "it is what it is"—no fault, no blame. I felt pain and compassion for their lives, too.

I decided to separate from Darrin and move back to Canada with our son. With or without our forgiveness, a dishonest marriage partner was unacceptable to me. I hugged and kissed him with pure love and empathy in my heart; I truly wished him well. I left with such peace. "Where God places you, you will not fail." Sometimes a dream has to die for a new dream to emerge.

When Darrin called three years later, I said, "Regardless of the outcome, you owe it to yourself and to me to tell the truth."

Within days of landing in Tennessee, I was in shock and sadness all over again. He revealed things to me that I could never

"When you harbor bitterness, happiness will dock elsewhere."

have imagined. But this time, it was different because I knew in my heart that he was willing to accept any outcome as the price for finally allowing himself to be authentic *no matter what.* That was *huge* for him! Now that we could start from a place of honesty, I decided to give our marriage another chance. Twenty-six years from the day we met, my soul mate and I are still together.

Through it all, I realized there is one thing that no one can ever take away from me: *my integrity!* I am so much richer now. Owning my own company provided me with a great public persona, a successful title and wealthy lifestyle. Strip away my wealth, my title and the letters after my name, and who am I? I don't worry about being successful; I continually work toward being *significant,* because where God places me, I will not fail! It's not the circumstance that matters; it's how we handle it that defines the difference.

No matter how hard or how many the blows that knock you down, God has a special plan and purpose for you and for each and every one of us. Where God places you, you truly will not fail!

Shelley Oglan is a brilliant speaker, certified coach, PeopleMap trainer and business development consultant. Her passion, authenticity, genuine support and practical application encourage individuals, professionals and teams to move forward by transforming ordinary communication into extraordinary results. Connect with Shelley at www.ShelleyOglan.com.

Destined to Fly

Jolene Roberts, RN

It looks like heaven: my plane resting idyllically above the clouds. Except now, I am no longer flying my plane. *Am I still alive? What are these bright lights, this soft angelic music and this new, light, floating feeling?* The scene is awe-inspiring. I feel exhilarated and at peace here. I hear familiar voices in the distance—they sound like the voices of my family and loved ones.

And then I wake up. *Where am I?* I feel utter despair to have left my beautiful place in the sky, and extremely frightened and confused. *Who am I? Has someone taken my brain?* I try to focus and am able to recognize my daughter, who is sitting next to me. She appears terrified, and tells me I was speaking about angels, but nothing else makes sense. I reach to console her, pulling her close and rocking her, but that is all I seem to be able to do. *I can't even remember my own name! Has someone done a lobotomy on me?*

Later, I would learn that I had come home from a flying session with a severe headache and distorted vision, and actually lapsed into a semi-comatose state. My husband, a physician himself, was in a state of shock and hesitated to heed advice from other physicians for twenty-four hours before finally bringing me to the hospital, where it was discovered that I had brain swelling brought on by systemic lupus cerebritis and nephritis. The diseases had also attacked my kidneys, thyroid and other organs.

Amazingly, I had survived—but the swelling had done severe damage to my brain, caused kidney failure and brought on an acute thyroid storm. When asked questions by physicians, I was unable to process them at all. Frustrated, scared and anxious, I cried and wondered, *Why won't my brain work?*

The shock of moving to the completely different culture of small-town, southwestern Altus, Oklahoma from Windsor, Ontario, Canada had been overwhelming. I felt utterly homesick and out of place in the foreign, oppressive desert environment, like a circular puzzle piece trying to fit into a square.

Studying and becoming proficient in aviation became an escape that helped me deal with the extreme stress of trying to acclimate to our new life and location. I became an accomplished

---

When asked questions by physicians, I was unable to process them at all.

---

pilot against tough odds, continued my career as an RN, raised my three beautiful kids and carved out a generally contented life for myself in what felt like an alien environment.

Flying to me meant freedom and individuality. Now, I was restricted from flying—grounded with what I saw as broken wings. I felt complete devastation at the loss of my former self! It was terrifying and awful to feel as though I no longer had a brain. I was searching for it, like the Scarecrow in *The Wizard of Oz.*

"The trauma from lupus cerebritis," the hospital doctors told me, "is like that from severe head injuries people experience in car accidents. The recovery period is very slow."

They were right. It was exceedingly slow. Numbers didn't make sense at all. I had always handled everything in our household, and now I couldn't even pay a bill! My new limitations terrified and saddened me. I suffered from night terrors, and every night at about four a.m. I woke up and vomited.

Still, because of my own medical background, the physicians' encouragement and our research, I knew recovery was possible.

My brain would eventually find new pathways where others had been destroyed. It would be a slow process, but I would just have to persevere and move forward. At least, I had my family and my faith. I found comfort in the Serenity Prayer every day.

It took almost a year for all my cognitive function to return, and another six months later we returned to Canada, so I could heal among family and friends. I underwent countless tests and scans, and was treated with myriad drugs, including heavy doses of cortisone injections and prednisone for four years, which caused me to gain a significant amount of weight. During my convalescence, I returned to the university to study psychology, women's studies and theology.

The one thing throughout my entire life that has been non-negotiable for me is my faith, and that strong Christian faith, combined with my inner fortitude, aided my healing process. The near-death experience in 1996 turned out to be a blessing in disguise, a sort of turning point when I reclaimed my body and my health and learned to fly in a different way as my physical, mental, psychological, emotional and spiritual well-being *all* improved, and I was finally able to fully return to life.

Before my illness, I had always been very physically active, but now the driving force that kept me disciplined was the idea that I was producing new, healthy cells that would devour my diseased ones. I was determined not to become a victim of the disease process, but there were definitely times of utter frustration and rivers of tears as I struggled to regain strength.

In September 2009, I joined a gym for the first time in ten years. We had planned a pilgrimage to Egypt and a climb up Mt. Sinai, so I trained rigorously. On our return home, I became ill with lupus complications and was again hospitalized. When I got back to the gym, the owners were anxious to view my pictures of Egypt. When they saw a picture of me in a bathing suit, they suggested I speak to my trainer, Jen, about being sponsored for a "fitness competition." The concept was foreign to me, and I merely laughed. Jen loved the idea, encouraged me to consider it and thought I had the muscle definition to qualify. I could not believe someone would be suggesting such an idea at my late age.

While attending the Fitness STAR International show, I approached the owner, James Erdt, to inquire about age categories. When he heard I was fifty, he convinced me to compete. Always inquisitive, I traveled to a workshop to see what fitness competitions were all about. On the drive home, I felt foolish and insecure about the desire to compete at my late age, but I also thought of one of the

---

I could not believe someone would be suggesting such an idea at my late age.

---

quotes I continue to live by: "You are never too old to set another goal or to dream a new dream!" *Lord,* I prayed, *I've been trying to do your Will since I almost died—if this isn't it, close the door.* A voice within said, *The way is paved.*

In March 2010, I stepped out on the stage for the first time—as the eldest contestant among seventy-five competitors. Although extremely nervous, I thoroughly enjoyed the experience. When they announced I had won first place, "Masters," I was ecstatic! How had I arrived at this place, with a medal around my neck? Suddenly, it dawned on me: I was flying again, but with both feet on the ground and mended wings!

St. Irenaeus said, "The glory of God is man fully alive." I feel so alive! I have grown through painful times, and my life has indeed been a blessed one. Adversity is a test of faith. When I dissected the word "faith," I found five words that describe my approach to life: F for faith, A for authenticity, I for integrity, T for tenacity and H for honor.

I am not sorry I became so ill; rather, I am thankful because of the way the experience has changed my views and awakened a new awareness in me of what is most important. Money, possessions and accomplishments mean very little if you do not have your health. I am grateful to God for humbling me in order for this to be revealed to me, and I am grateful for the opportunity to have the courage, strength, determination and focus to live a life that makes a difference and to share it with the world.

Many people have been inspired by my story: "Wow, if she can do it, why can't I?"

They've actually watched me beat my disease—for example, at the gym this summer when I was extremely ill and could not breathe at all. At that time, when I was up for an inspirational award, people told me, "Amazing. We watched you from the sidelines with your inhaler. While somebody else may have quit and stayed in bed, it just motivated you to keep moving." Because of my age and the adversities I've faced, people see their own potential in me.

Now I am thrilled to be part of a new realm of like-minded people who are determined to achieve the best performance with the bodies they have been blessed with. Many people remain grudging about taking care of their health or begrudge their lack

We're only given one body in this lifetime.

of it. But, we're only given one body in this lifetime. We treat our family, pets and possessions lovingly but fail to treat ourselves the same way.

I truly believe that for a successful flight in life, and to fully mend your broken wings, you must treat your body, your mind, your heart and your spirit with the same loving care. Then you will be equipped to visualize your goal or purpose and strive to stay focused until it is accomplished. Never let thoughts, uncertainties or other people's opinions obstruct the final outcome! Trust in the life unfolding within you and allow your soul to have a voice! Your own true story is your own script, and maturity has much less to do with the years you have lived than what you have done with knowledge gained from your own experience.

Jolene Roberts's life achievements are numerous: She is a mother, RN, pilot, leader, counselor, volunteer, champion fitness competitor and model, inspirational and motivational fitness coach, published author, regularly-featured radio guest and public speaker. Connect with Jolene and learn more about overcoming adversity at www.Faith-and-Fitness.com.

In Order to Blossom

Teresa Surya Ma McKee

I t's the unexpected joys that are the true success stories of our lives.

This one was really something special. It had been such a journey—and for a long time, such a struggle—to arrive here, using my own key to unlock the front door, and swing it open for the very first time onto the airy rectangle I was about to transform into my dream, my center.

Isn't it interesting that the universe has given me a second chance? My space waited for me as a blank canvas waits for the painter's brush. *I can create whatever I want to create here,* I thought. *What a breath of fresh air. The possibilities are endless—it's time to get to work!* But just two years earlier . . .

"I don't understand. What do you mean, someone else has signed the contract? I've put so much time into this! Do you understand the amount of work and research I've done to prepare myself for this? This is my dream! What am I supposed to do now?"

While teaching yoga and providing alternative therapies in my local community, I'd been preparing to become Knoxville, Tennessee's Migun distributor of wellness products. I had been established in the community for over fifteen years; I had done the research and the soul-searching, I had put the money together. Now I was ready to take my stand for holistic health as a business owner. My vision looked more and more like a reality with each excitement-filled passing day—until the rug was ripped out from under my feet when I called Migun's offices to touch base.

I was told that someone else had signed a contract to handle "my" territory and was actually moving to the area to start the business. Apparently, part of my new-distributor application had fallen through the cracks somewhere, and in the meantime, the territory had been signed away to someone else. I couldn't believe it. I felt so betrayed. Was this all some cruel joke to get my hopes up, and then dash them?

Allowing myself a three-day "pissed-off party" spent in self-imposed solitary confinement, I raged over what I believed to be a bad business decision. I was not willing to compromise my life and role in the community to move to another area of the country to continue chasing the dream I was beginning to doubt. *What*

---

*I felt so betrayed. Was this all some cruel joke
to get my hopes up, and then dash them?*

---

was the company doing, contracting someone from another city that would have welcomed the service and support, when I was ready and willing right here? The new distributor could stay in their city and both areas would be served. How can I see this so clearly and understand that this is how I'm supposed to serve the community, yet have this insurmountable obstacle placed in my path? The contract had already been signed. There was no changing it.

After those three days, my temper tantrum was over. I released the desire and need to be right, even though I had followed correct procedure and believed I was justified in feeling wronged and upset. Despite feeling misled by the universe, I chose to put my spiritual philosophy into practice and reach for the higher thought. It was time to put my big girl panties on and embrace the possibility that there was more in store for me.

In other words, it was time to get over myself and act like a grown-up.

Most significantly, it was during this time that I was able to put into practice the biggest lesson I had learned so far: Letting go of attachment to outcome. The theory is to begin with the end in mind, do your prep work and let the pieces fall where they may. When things don't seem to go your way, let go of your idea of how things should be.

Through the years that followed, I authentically and truly supported the store under other ownership. This approach did not fail me: Two years after my huge letdown, I stepped forward

This time was just the right time.

and took over the store. I was able to sublease the space from the owner and have my own distributorship with the company. The territory was now mine and I recognized that having the Migun store coupled with my health and wellness center was a great thing for our community.

My husband and I came up with a three-year business plan that covered the Migun branding in year one, branding Integrative Synergy in year two, and personal branding in year three so that I could become a national keynote speaker and workshop conductor.

I had spent so long waiting for this opportunity, and then had completely given up on it, that I was surprised when the opportunity presented itself again. I decided to go for it—again. I just couldn't wait to make my vision a reality. And because I had been so deeply disappointed the first time I lost my dream, I was exponentially more grateful when it finally did come true. I hit the ground running, and poured my entire heart and soul into bringing the center's potential to fruition. This time was just the right time.

We pre-launched the center with a cleansing breathwork intensive by Babaji from the Kashi Center for Advanced Spiritual Studies, even before we brought in all the equipment and product. It cleared the leftover energy in the space from the previous occupant's work and vision that just didn't gel with what we wanted to do. I had a wonderful Feng Shui master set the store energetically and dust the negativity from my blank canvas. We did this to create a loving, healing, wonderful space—which is exactly what it became.

I had the opportunity to coordinate many workshops and classes at the center with healers and professionals from all over the country. Learning with and from them gave me a lot of knowledge and training that I was able to integrate into my business plan.

Dreams must be allowed to grow
organically in order for them to blossom.

I can't help but smile and shake my head now at my early rage and impatience. But of course I didn't know, back then, that all of my hard work had not been in vain. The wonderful surprise is the knowing that, without being forced into taking the long way around, I might never have learned that dreams must be allowed to grow organically in order for them to blossom.

By fearlessly letting go of my attachment to a specific outcome and precisely the path I had seen myself walking, I let myself surrender to and trust the universe—a big thing for a recovering perfectionist! Yet, I did it, and things opened up so beautifully that now, I can look back on one of the most turbulent and confidence-shattering times of my life and greet it like an old friend that helped me move toward my true purpose.

We all have our dreams. They give us drive, they motivate us, they help us get up in the morning. Most of us need them to keep us focused and striving for greatness in our lives. But, sometimes we need to give them a little air and sun to let them blossom in fullness.

What could the universe have in store for you? What if—just what if—it's something even better, more magical, more fulfilling, more exciting than the dream you're dreaming now?

TERESA SURYA MA MCKEE

Teresa Surya Ma McKee is a visionary teacher who encourages dreamers, healers, leaders and their communities to show up fully in the world, bringing their essence into action. Her passion is to share with individuals, organizations and communities how to dream again... to have hope for the future... one dream at a time.

The author of numerous articles on stress, energy medicine, yoga, breathwork and aromatherapy, Teresa teaches and coordinates workshops and events nationally. She is a featured visionary in the book Fearless Women: Visions of a New World, *a co-owner of the True Purpose™ Institute, and serves on the Founder's Circle for the Million Dreams Campaign, which is an initiative of Dream University®. She is a member of the Kashi Institute for Advanced Spiritual Studies and is a student of Ma Jaya. Teresa's background in clinical aromatherapy, Healing Touch Spiritual Ministry, Kali Natha Yoga and breathwork has greatly influenced her integrative energy medicine practice. She is a Dream Coach®, stress coach, and is soon to become a health coach through the Institute of Integrative Nutrition. Teresa is past President of Healing Touch East Tennessee, and has served on the board of CHEO, the Complementary Health Education Organization. Connect with Teresa at www.IntegrativeSynergy.com .*

Conclusion

Sandra Yancey

In the introduction, I shared the story about the time when, after two years of burning the candle at both ends and still coming up short, I seriously considered shifting my primary focus away from eWomenNetwork so that I would have time to get a job. Ultimately, my mother's wisdom—"How do you know you're not quitting five minutes before the miracle begins?"—helped me to see that I couldn't give up.

It was during this challenging time that my daughter Briana, eight years old at the time, was invited to go to Six Flags, an amusement park similar to Disneyland. I not only didn't have the money to pay for the entrance fee, I didn't even have the extra spending money to give her so that she could buy something to drink.

I had so much pride, and at that age kids repeat a lot of things we don't want others to hear, such as "I can't afford it." I feared she would say to her friend, "I can't go because my mommy can't afford it," so instead I said, "Oh, Briana, you can't go because I have a huge surprise planned for you today!"

Briana's eyes lit up and she said, "What's the surprise?"

Stalling until I could come up with an answer, I replied, "Have you made your bed?"

When she shook her head "no," I immediately responded, "Go make your bed and then I'll tell you."

She ran up the stairs and I walked into the pantry, looking for ideas. I'm not even sure why I walked into the pantry; it was just nervous energy. I was thinking, *What am I going to do? What am I going to do?* As I looked at the top shelf, I spotted the box where I kept the leftover birthday party supplies—crepe paper, party hats, and the like.

I pulled the box down and found a bag of balloons. Then I thought, *One of her most favorite things in the world is playing with water balloons.* So, I started filling water balloons, stacking them in a cooler. When Briana came downstairs, I said, "We're going to

> They transformed their setbacks
> into steppingstones.

go out and have a water balloon fight, just the two of us. And then we're going to have a great lunch." At the time, Briana's favorite lunch was boxed macaroni and cheese, mixed with hot dogs cut up to look like coins, so, inspite of our limited budget, it was easy to give her a fantastic day.

The answers to your questions and the solutions to your problems aren't always to find or spend more money, or to change who you are. The solution begins with making the most of what's really important to you, not accepting your perceived limitations as truth, and then asking for help.

About ten years later, Briana was graduating from National Charity League, a six-year program in which mothers teach their daughters about philanthropy. At the end of the six years, when the girls are seniors in high school, they have a big graduation with all of the pomp and circumstance. The girls wear beautiful dresses that look like wedding gowns and their fathers present them with a video montage, which plays behind them. For the video, the girls pick twenty photos that represent the evolution of their life and the lessons they've learned.

I was traveling when Briana chose her photos, and when I got home she said, "I have a stack of photos and I want you to look through them and tell me if I'm missing something significant."

As I leafed through the pictures, I couldn't believe what I found. Out of all of the gazillion photos she had to choose from, she picked one of the pictures I took of her that day we played with the water balloons. Suddenly I realized, *Here I thought I was just trying to make do and keep from disappointing Briana, and to shield myself from the embarrassment of people finding out that I was so broke I couldn't afford to send her to Six Flags, and really I had created a special memory that my daughter treasured.*

In every story in this book, the co-authors accepted their situation and made the most of what they had. They embraced challenges and change and welcomed even the hardest, most painful lessons as an opportunity to become more of who they really are. They transformed their setbacks into steppingstones, and in some cases, succeeded, not just *in spite of* everything, but *because* of everything.

You have your own struggles. Perhaps, as I once was, you are just starting out and are working long hours to make a go of your business. Or maybe life just happened; maybe you're dealing with unexpected twists, turns or obstacles that seem impossible to navigate or overcome. Take comfort in these stories in this book, so that you know you're not alone, and then let them inspire you to get creative and take *action.*

As you close the last page on this book, I invite you to take a deep breath, then another, and when you stand up, put one arm and fist in the air and shout, "CHARGE!" I challenge you to go for it, to carry on in a big, audacious, amazing way! You deserve to create a powerful, successful, happy life… you deserve your dream!

About Sandra Yancey

Sandra Yancey, an award-winning entrepreneur, international business owner, author, movie producer, speaker and philanthropist who has been recognized by CNN as an American Hero, is dedicated to helping women achieve and succeed. She is the founder and CEO of eWomenNetwork, a multi-million dollar enterprise recognized as the premier women's business network in North America.

Sandra is the author of *Relationship Networking* and, co-authored with Julie Ziglar Norman, *Mastering Moxie: From Contemplating to Creating Absolute Success.* She is also featured in *Chicken Soup for the Entrepreneur's Soul,* which showcases some of the top entrepreneurs in North America.

Connect with Sandra and the other co-authors and learn about the eWomenNetwork at www.eWomenNetwork.com.

We invite you to experience the
Succeeding In Spite Of Everything
MULTIMEDIA book.

Now that you've read these amazing stories, you can also view the online version of *SUCCEEDING IN SPITE OF EVERYTHING* on your computer or iPad in an exciting, next-generation multimedia format.

Adding AUDIO and VIDEO conversations to the text, the co-authors share more knowledge and inspiration to help you turn the obstacles in your life into triumphs.

We offer you a GIFT of several chapters from the
Succeeding In Spite of Everything
multimedia book at:

www.SucceedingInSpite.com

If you wish to buy the complete multimedia book, please use this coupon code to receive a substantial discount.

Coupon Code — Book9

We also invite you to share your thoughts about our book with our community on our Facebook page at:

www.Facebook.com/eWomenNetwork

We invite you to read and experience several free chapters of other Yinspire Media multimedia books. If you wish to by the complete multimedia books, we invite you to use the coupon codes to receive a substantial discount. You can purchase the print versions of all these books at Amazon.com.

Unbreakable Spirit
Rising Above the Impossible
www.UnbreakableSpiritBook.com
Coupon Code – Book8

Get Your Woman On
Embracing Beauty, Grace & The Power of Women
www.GetYourWomanOnBook.com
Coupon Code – Book7

Fight For Your Dreams
The Power of Never Giving Up
www.Fight4YourDreams.com
Coupon Code – Book6

Living Proof
Celebrating the Gifts that Came Wrapped in Sandpaper
www.LivingProofMBook.com
Coupon Code – Book5

How Did You Do That!
Stories of Going for IT
www.HowDidUDoThat.com
Coupon Code – Book2

The Law of Business Attraction
Secrets of Cooperative Success
www.LawOfBusinessAttraction.com
Coupon Code – Book1

The Wealth Garden
The New Dynamics of Wealth Creation in a Fast-Changing Global Economy
www.WealthGardenBook.com
Coupon Code – Book 3

Transforming Through 2012
Leading Perspectives on the New Global Paradigm
www.2012MultimediaEbook.com
Coupon Code – Book 4